No More Hiding
A Tale of Two Beasts

BY TIMOTHY SAWYER

No More Hiding
A Tale of Two Beasts

TIMOTHY SAWYER

StoryTerrace

Text Patricia West, on behalf of StoryTerrace

Design Mitar Stjepcevic, on behalf of StoryTerrace

Copyright © Timothy Sawyer and StoryTerrace

Text is private and confidential

First print April 2022

StoryTerrace

www.StoryTerrace.com

CONTENTS

PART ONE
A ROUGH START

"Drugs take you to hell, disguised as heaven."
—Donald Lyn Frost

1

INTRODUCTION

The Bad Beast

I n 1986, at the age of nineteen, my teenage reign as a complete drain on society ended abruptly when the police raided my apartment.

Large Dealers Nabbed, Police Say

FRAMINGHAM—Two eighteen-year-olds, characterized by police as "large street dealers," were arrested over the weekend in a drug raid that yielded cocaine, marijuana, cash, and drug paraphernalia.

After receiving complaints from neighbors of a suspicious amount of both foot and car traffic, police raided 78A Summer St. Saturday night, according to Lt. Brent Larrabee.

Arrested at that time was Robert Lopez, 78A Summer St., who was charged with possession of cocaine with intent to distribute, possession of marijuana with intent to distribute, and illegal possession of LSD, according to police records.

Arrested Sunday night was Timothy C. Sawyer, also of 78A Summer St. He was charged with possession of cocaine with intent to distribute, possession of marijuana with intent to distribute, possession of LSD and conspiracy to violate the narcotics laws, according to police records.

Larrabee described Lopez and Sawyer as "two major pushers of marijuana and cocaine in Framingham." He added, "We consider this a significant arrest. They are both considered large street dealers."

Excerpt from the Middlesex News, February 1985

You see, my roommate and I were drug dealers. We sold a cadre of drugs with a primary focus on cocaine. We were well-known to the police, who constantly sent people into our apartment in an attempt to catch us dealing. Unfortunately, we were pretty vigilant about avoiding that scheme, but we loved to taunt the police. If I saw a car and thought it might be an undercover cop, which it was many times, I would take my pit bull terrier outside, walk towards the car, light a cigarette, and just stand there staring off into space. They would leave, and I would get in my car and try to follow them back to the police station. Of course, it didn't end well; they raided our apartment and confiscated everything. I had already been arrested several times for a series of crimes, including breaking and entering, larceny, driving to endanger, and—get this—breaking *into* a police station!

After the raid, the DA pressed for a ten-year sentence in Walpole State Prison for Men. As this would have been my first actual prison sentence, I would have to serve one year before being eligible for parole—one tenth of the sentence. I was six feet tall, weighed 145 pounds, strung out, and terrified because Walpole is a tough state prison where many of the inmates are never getting out. Call me a coward, but my life would not have gone in the direction it did if it wasn't for my father's relentless advocacy and willingness to support me in and out of the courtroom. My dad had no reason to believe in me, but he never gave up. In the end, I caught a big break; the judge remanded me to a one-year residential drug treatment program with probation and a two-and-a-half-year suspended sentence. I'm not a big fan of moral victories; however, this is one I would take. I never did cocaine again, but I am still an addict who found a way to redirect my compulsions.

So begins my tale of two beasts, commonly referred to as the battle between the good wolf and the bad wolf according to the old Cherokee legend. Years later, when I admitted my criminal record to my children, I shared the story with them:

One day an elder Indian talked to his grandson about the struggle between good and evil and told him we all have two wolves inside us. One represents everything bad, the other represents everything good, and they are always fighting.

So, the grandson said, "Well, how do you decide who wins?" and the grandfather said, "It's the one you feed the most."

Moving On

Although I continue to struggle with my inner beasts, my life has changed dramatically since my arrest in 1986. I quit drugs, completed college, and married my soulmate, who still amazes me after 30 years. In my first job after working for my father, I quickly realized I was very good at two things: sales and teaching people how to sell. There was just one problem: I had to overcome my paralyzing fear of public speaking to move ahead. And I did. Despite twelve years of service as a top producer, manager, and corporate trainer, I was terminated as a result of good old-fashioned nepotism and learned my first real lesson about the Golden Rule: "He who has the gold; rules." That termination led to a major turning point in my life.

I vowed to do whatever I had to do to avoid being in that position again. I had learned a harsh lesson: No Equity = No Deal. I took my family on a cross-country RV trip, recording my thoughts and feelings while deciding what to do. Over the next two years, I took time to regroup and re-assess. I received income from a one-year non-compete with the bank, made some money flipping houses, and started a consulting business. I also met an amazing dude named

Adam, a successful entrepreneur who eventually approached me about starting a company together. Ultimately, Adam and I co-founded two companies that made it to the INC 500. Both were a financial success, but this was all new to me, and the emotional cost was high. My inner beasts were often at war through the pressure and the challenges. Work was often my priority, and my family, health, and even my faith suffered because of my choices. Like any partnership, Adam and I often dealt with each other's shifting priorities. We sold the first company in 2011 and the second in 2020.

Thanks to the commercial success of those enterprises, my wife and I now live in a home on the water where we enjoy the sights of seals sunning on rocks from our windows. We have three beautiful children who are all doing well. Professionally, I am an established motivational speaker, author, entrepreneur, and hopefully a trusted professional. While the journey has been a long, strange road, those who know me well know this about me; if I tell you it's raining, you don't need to put your hand out the window.

None of this would be possible without the support of my wife and my family. On the way, I met great people who forever changed the way I look at life, including a fascinating stranger at an RV park in Albuquerque, New Mexico. After the sale of our last venture, I felt like it was time to reflect, regroup again, and think about the next chapter of my life. I'm sure this will be an evolving story. Self-discovery is a never-ending journey. In the beginning, I screwed up badly.

I hurt a lot of good people, and I own that. But it's not over, and I'm ready to increase my efforts toward giving back.

Why am I writing this? We all make mistakes. Starting life as a drug dealer and convicted felon at eighteen was not what I had hoped for, but that's where I was. My goals for this book are, first and foremost, to remind us all that "it's never fatal 'til it's fatal." I leaned on that concept many times. I want to inspire young entrepreneurs to pursue their dreams while understanding the trade-offs. I want them to know that anything is possible, and we all struggle along the way. Success and failure are not permanent states, and for those who suffer from occasional lack of confidence, low self-esteem, and fear of failure—the past does not have to define them. I also want them to recognize the importance of people in their lives, understanding that none of us is perfect and that you can't love half a person; you must love the whole person, including the good and bad beasts who battle within.

2

GROWING UP IN FRAMINGHAM

My Town

I was born in Lynn, Massachusetts, and grew up in Framingham, about twenty miles west of Boston. We lived in a typical three-bedroom, one-and-a-half-bathroom ranch house my dad bought for $26,700 in a middle-class neighborhood. I was the middle child of three boys—Tom, me, and Todd—and shared a bedroom with Todd, my younger brother by four years. We lived in a horseshoe-shaped development of ranch houses in a neighborhood full of diverse families. It was like a scene from the movie *Sand Lot*.

I was a child of the '60s and the '70s. In those days, there were no playdates, credit checks on your neighbors, or social media, and kids in the neighborhood were outside when not in school. We had a great neighborhood, and I had a group of fifteen or so friends there. We were always outside playing sports or games like kickball, dodgeball, or thanks for the beacon. My brother Tom was always involved and Todd tagged along as much as possible. Tom was our protector. If we had a problem with someone in the neighborhood, he was ready, willing, and able to solve it. Tom was always comfortable throwing the first punch when conflict was inevitable; a tendency that would be both a blessing and a curse for him as we grew older. Both of my brothers were the kind of guys who ran toward the fight. My younger brother, Todd, joined the 82nd Airborne. He was brave—not the kind of bravery it takes to start a business, the kind of bravery I admired. The kind that says sleep well tonight, I got you. After the army and a successful career in tech, Todd became a pastor, amateur UFC trainer, and fitness coach. Tom is also a successful business owner, tech guru, and avid triathlete.

Family History

I had a DNA test done through an online site and discovered that I am over 90% English. Hence, the constant sunburns, I guess.

I never knew my great-grandparents, but I did spend time with my paternal and maternal grandparents. My dad's family lived in rural Maine, and my mom's family in suburbanMassachusetts. The two families could not have been more different, but each valued family and tried to stay close.

Paternal Grandparents

My father's parents, Everett and Ruth Sawyer, had rural roots in Central Maine. When I visited them with my parents as a young man, they lived in a farmhouse that would one day be condemned. The old farmhouse had a beat-up tin roof, a dilapidated front porch, no running water, and an outhouse for a bathroom. But it was surrounded by twenty acres of land, and the rent was only $45 a month. My dad's family consisted of thirteen children. As my dad would say, though, it wasn't bad because a new sibling would be born as the oldest moved out. So, on average, there were only six or seven living at home at any one time. The family moved often because they couldn't afford to pay the rent. When they lived on a farm in Rome, Maine, the children walked a mile to a one-room schoolhouse. Every day started with the pledge of allegiance to the flag and singing by the piano. Each row of students represented a grade, and the row setup enabled my dad to skip one grade because he paid attention to the material taught to the older kids in the row behind him. My dad has always been the caretaker type, and he helped maintain the school by sweeping the floors, starting the old wood furnace, and thawing out the drinking water in the ceramic urn. He was paid $1.50 a week for his efforts. Dad used to buy strawberry plants so the family could sell the fruit.

In a typical photo of my grandfather, you would see him covered in dirt from head to toe and wearing a farmer's hat. Grandpa Sawyer didn't work a conventional job; the story is that a tree fell on him early in life, and he was never the same after that. He was a rough character, a hard-core farmer. He could be a mean dude who struggled with the pressure of feeding his large brood. Every sentence Grandpa spoke would be laced with colorful language, which drove my mother crazy. All Grandpa did was hunt, fish, grow vegetables, and look for his next odd job. Even though there was a five-fish legal limit, Grandpa would go into the woods, find a stream, cut an alder sapling for a fishing pole, grab a fishline/hook from his pocket and start catching as many brook trout as was needed to feed his family. Sometimes he filled his ragged old coat pockets with as many as 50 small trout. Grandpa didn't say much, but when he did, he just walked into the room, nodded, and started rambling on about Saturday night dancing with Grandma, hunting, fishing, and his pet dog, Freckles, while the aroma from his corn-cob pipe, packed with George Washington tobacco, filled the room.

My father reluctantly told me a story about his best Christmas ever. The family only ate what they shot or grew, and one year, Grandpa Sawyer poached a deer out of season. As a result, he was arrested and locked up, and DCYF (Division for Children, Youth, and Families) was contacted. They came out to the house, saw the poor living conditions, and arranged for the children to have new mittens, boots, and jackets—things they had never had. My father said it was the greatest Christmas ever. Everyone was so excited, and Grandpa was "only" locked up for a short time.

Grandma Sawyer was cool—always fun, pleasant, and willing to chat with you. She did tend to be preoccupied with subjects such as her little garden or her newest boyfriend. Grandma and Grandpa had a non-traditional relationship. My grandmother always wanted more. She loved a lot, which sometimes led to some awkward situations for her and her children. Grandma and Grandpa parted ways in their mid-60s, with Grandma heading back to her roots in Somerville, Massachusetts, and Grandpa moving to an old, dilapidated two-room cabin in the woods of Maine. We didn't see Grandpa much after that. But my father stayed close with his mom until she died, and we visited her apartment frequently.

Aunt Mary's Farm: The Purest Form of Childhood

As I said, most of my dad's family is from rural Maine. I often spent time on a farm with my father's sister Mary, where she and her husband, Ken, raised cows, bulls, pigs, and chickens. Mary and Ken had eight children, and my brothers and I were close to the middle kids who were nearest to us in age. During the summer, I would spend one or two weeks a year on the farm, and those days are among my happiest memories of growing up. We could fish in the frog pond, fool around with the animals, and jump in the hay. There were lakes all around us, and we swam often.

The farm's frog pond was across the street from the house, and we would earn money to pay for our annual trip to the Skowhegan State Fair by catching frogs and pulling worms from the cow pastures. A baby frog was worth three cents, and a worm was worth a penny. We did that all week, making ten or twelve dollars, enough to have a blast at the fair. We would stand in the water and face the bank to catch frogs because the frogs would jump in from the bank when startled. We would walk back to the house when we were done, and Aunt Mary would scrape the leeches off our bodies. We would bleed for a few minutes, harmlessly, but we didn't care. Hey, frogs were three cents apiece, and I was only eleven. Little did I know I had already caught the sales bug. Think about it; if you go into a pond to catch frogs, knowing you would be covered with leeches and doing it anyway, you might be a little tapped.

We also enjoyed tipping cows over at night and harassing bulls. We would sneak up to the big barn, where the cows had fallen asleep standing up, and would push them over. The craziest thing we did was to get in the pen with a bull, rile it up, and then let it chase us into the electric fencing. The goal was to get under the fence before the bull reached us;

nine times out of ten, we ended up with burns on our backs from the electric fence. Sounds crazy unless you're crazy.

When I look back on my life, there weren't many times I can say I had good, clean, fun, but visits to Aunt Mary's farm fit that bill.

Maternal Grandparents

My maternal grandparents were Roderick and Letha McLean, who lived in suburban Massachusetts. They had five children, four girls and one boy. Grandpa McLean was a house painter who smoked constantly and had a yard full of junk, but he enjoyed walking through the debris with me and telling me what it was. Unlike my father's dad, Grandpa McLean was an easy-going guy. I remember him as gentle, loving, and funny. I only visited my dad's parents once or twice, but I spent a lot of time with Grandpa and Grandma McLean.

The McLean house was a slight upgrade compared with that of my father's parents. There were creaky floors, an old laminate floor in the kitchen, old furniture, and one TV in their tiny living room. The only bathroom in the small, two-bedroom home seldom worked correctly. The front door was on the side, not facing the street, and the front part of their house was strange; the foundation came up about eight feet off the ground, and it looked like they had cut off the front part of the house. My grandfather loved to collect junk. And he had a lot of it.

My brothers and I spent many Sundays at church with my mother and grandmother, followed by a visit and lunch. Grandma McLean was a devout Christian and raised her children in the church. Grandfather did not attend church much, but he was a good father; he and Grandma stayed close to all their children.

My mother was generous and kind. She would be content to sit and chat and take us with her when she went out. She taught other people to sew and clean houses.

When I was a kid, we mostly spent Christmas with my mother's side of the family, and there was lots of love and, at times, also a lot of drinking. My Aunt Roberta (one of Mom's sisters), who I loved, and her husband, Uncle Billy, owned a couple of rough bars in Revere Beach that mainly catered to biker types—hard people. We celebrated Christmas at a table in the back for years while the bar remained open, and one of my cousins would get up occasionally to serve the guests. The bar also contained a pinball machine and darts, which my cousin Marty would allow us to play for free, which worked for us.

Uncle Billy was a tough guy. Nobody messed with him. He and Aunt Roberta had four children, my first cousins, and three of them died early. Billy Jr. was killed crossing a street in Revere when a drunk driver hit him. He was only 27 years old. Marty and Donna both died from complications related to alcohol. Marty had severe cirrhosis of the liver. He was a big, outgoing, life-of-the-party tough guy who spent much of his life as a bouncer, bartender, and cook. I liked Marty a lot, as did everyone else. He was my family hero, a larger-than-life guy who always made me feel like one of the cool guys.

Sadly, alcohol and drugs were rampant in my family. One of Mom's sisters struggled with substance abuse for most of her life until she became sober about fifteen years before her death. My Uncle Bobby, the youngest of my mom's four siblings, also had a severe drinking problem. He died of cirrhosis of the liver, was homeless towards the end of his life, and was another guy who was always doing crazy things. One time he was pulled over by a police officer for driving erratically, and then—after the officer got out of his car—Bobby jumped into it and took off. My uncle actually stole the police car.

Parents

My parents, Thomas and Kathleen Sawyer, met in Lynn, Massachusetts, where Dad was working in an automotive parts store when my mother walked in to apply for a job in the office. It wasn't long before Dad was buying her a morning coffee and a muffin and meeting at the time clock. And as they say, the rest is history. My parents never had a traditional wedding. They eloped. They were very young, very much in love, and might have gotten a little ahead of themselves.

Father

My dad left Maine at seventeen and headed for Massachusetts. He lived with his sister, June, and her husband, Bernard, in an apartment in Lynn and worked at a drugstore before working for the Automotive Parts Company. After that, he landed a job at American Finance company, making personal loans. He and my mother married, and as the family grew, he moved us to Framingham to work at Marlboro Savings Bank, where he was hired to start a new loan department and develop the bank's marketing program. Eventually, my dad left that job to become the marketing manager at a daily newspaper in Milford, Massachusetts.

The paper's publisher was a talented Dartmouth College grad with an excessive drinking problem. My dad befriended him, worked hard, and was promoted to assistant to the publisher. As a result, the publisher became an advocate for my dad, and when he died, the paper's owners promoted my dad to general manager and eventually publisher, even though he would have been third or fourth in line for the job. My father heavily invested in the community as a fundraiser, philanthropist, and perennial volunteer. His hard work and sense of community were rewarded with an invitation to become an influential board member of a community bank, a position he held for decades until the bank was sold.

My father was self-taught, worked hard, and took advantage of every opportunity that came his way. He was a great team player. No job was below him; if a photographer were out sick, he would hop in his car and shoot a picture himself. Dad was also a humble and frugal guy, and when it came to money, my dad had two moves—to give it away or save it. The giveaway part stuck with me, the saving part not so much. Saving my money was a lesson I never learned and eventually paid for dearly.

My dad gave everything to the community, and people loved him. He became president of his local Rotary Club and trustee of the local hospital, and he received several community awards. In addition, he was president of the town soccer club and coached for many years.

My dad was also a somewhat overscheduled control freak. Unfortunately, I don't think that always worked for everyone.

Mother

My mother was raised in the church. Like her mother, her faith influenced all aspects of her life. While growing up, my mom would make sure we attended church with her. But, for the most part, she was happiest as a wife and homemaker. Occasionally, she worked as a house cleaner, a server at a donut shop, and at sub shops—whatever she could find. Her favorite job was working at a Chinese restaurant as a hostess.

My mother worked hard and did everything she could to care for us. Later in life, she earned her CNA (certified nurse's assistant) license and worked in private care and nursing homes. Mom also worked as a part-time activities director at many nursing homes. Sadly, her mother, who had been diagnosed with Alzheimer's, spent her last years in a nursing home, a 30-minute drive each way for my mother. But Mom made the trip almost every day for thirteen years, helping to care for Grandma until she died. Mom was thankful for the help from her two sisters.

My parents could be best described as devoted husband and wife, ultra-conservative, right-wing Christians. My mother now works with the elderly and sings in the small choir at the church where my younger brother Todd is a pastor. Like many in her generation, she now takes pride in her role of doting wife, mother, grandmother, and great-grandmother.

Mom, Dad, Tommy and me. My Dad loved to referee youth football games

Grampa Sawyer outside his farmhouse in Maine

Outside our Framingham home after the blizzard of '78

My and my little brother Todd

Ice fishing with my best friend Peter

Outside Grampa McLean's home in Saugus, MA

My Mom taking care of Grandma McLean

Me, Tommy and Todd in Framingham

Mom and the boys

My home growing up in Framingham, MA

3

DRUG USER TO DRUG DEALER: A SHORT WALK

In the Beginning

'll never forget the first time I did drugs. I was walking home from school with a friend, and he told me he had some marijuana. We didn't have any rolling papers or a pipe, so we put it inside a semi-plastic shoelace thing and fired it up. We were only twelve years old, not very sophisticated at the time. By the time I was thirteen, I was smoking pot, drinking, and getting into big-time trouble. I was failing all my classes and only going to school three or four days a week, and my mother was constantly getting phone calls from school truant officers. In middle school, my friend Peter and I were so brazen that we would skip school and go ice fishing across the street from the school. Students and teachers could look out the window and see us there, fishing and smoking pot. By the time I was a sophomore in high school, I was in remedial reading and math classes and print shop, and I had zero interest in school.

My relationship with drugs and alcohol was a match made in hell from the start. I was off to the races from hello. I was given a lot of leeway as a teenager and used the freedom to get drunk and high whenever I could. My friend Peter and I were two peas in a pod. I would tell my parents, "I'm going to Peter's for the weekend," which was fine with them. I wasn't close to my dad at the time, but I developed a close relationship with Peter's dad, a detective, and we did everything together. I went to all his hockey games, he came to my soccer games, and we went fishing together. Unfortunately, his dad was also a serious drinker, and that's where Peter and I learned to party. Peter's parents often had big get-togethers, and we could easily grab a six-pack and hang out for hours in their detached garage. We were twelve at the time.

Peter and I were always looking for ways to get into trouble. We both had a newspaper route when we were fourteen or fifteen, and Peter had a moped—big trouble. I had discovered cocaine by then. Peter wasn't a huge fan at first, but we would smoke some pot, grab my newspapers, deliver them on his moped, and then go back to his house to deliver his newspapers. Occasionally, we would take off on the moped late at night to cause trouble. We were pyromaniacs, constantly lighting the woods or tires on fire. The police would come, and we would run, only to sneak back to watch them deal with our fire. Once the police were gone, we would do it again—the same night. We did other stupid things that could have led to hurting people, like throwing tomatoes or snowballs at cars. I can't tell you how many times people chased us. We never got caught, but we came close a couple of times. Anything to fuel my need for constant adrenaline. Even then, at fourteen, I was wired to take risks, but I was still feeding the bad beast.

A Different Generation of Parenting

In the 1980s, parenting was a different gig than it is now. Parents were busy. My mom had her thing going on, and my overscheduled dad was just trying to keep it together. And it wasn't like things weren't going wrong. When I was ten or eleven years old, I started shoplifting. The first time I got caught, I shoplifted Pop Rocks from Zayre's, where my mom worked in the store diner. As the insanity progressed, I would leave razor blades in my pants pockets from cutting the coke. My mom did the laundry, found them, and asked me what they were doing there. I would say something like, "Oh, I use them for shop class." No one did or said anything. I don't know if it was blind faith or a blind eye, but that was the prevailing "model" at the time—at least as far as I knew.

My parents weren't the only adults who seemed comfortable with teens doing their thing. I began to date at an early age, having sex, getting high, and drinking with my girlfriends in their homes. Their parents weren't around or failed to check on us. I dated my first girlfriend in the sixth grade for a year or two, and we used to steal pot from her parents' dresser drawers. Her parents would go out, leaving us alone to do whatever we wanted.

I gravitated towards girls from families with money at a young age, and I became obsessed with nice things. For the most part, these girls were obsessed with bad dudes. Their parents might be doctors or lawyers, and their lives were very different from mine, but I could influence them to do insane things. Sometimes we had terrible drug experiences, and one of the scariest involved my high school girlfriend. We were smoking pot in her garage, and suddenly her eyes rolled back into her head, and she fell unconscious, hitting her head on the concrete floor. Fortunately, she was OK, with a minor cut on her head. Unfortunately, this was the first of many self-inflicted injuries I would see and be a part of over the next few years. My girlfriend's injury was nothing compared to some that came later.

There was one house my friends and I could go to any night of the week, where anything went—the home of my friend Bill. His dad didn't care what we did and went to bed at eight o'clock, and his mother worked nights as a nurse. So, my friends and I would stay up all night, smoking cigarettes and marijuana, snorting coke, drinking alcohol, and watching porn in the basement. Neither of Bill's parents smoked, so they could surely smell our cigarettes and pot, but if his mother tried to say something, Bill would tell her to shut up. She would reply, "Well, Billy, don't stay up all night," and then leave for work. I'm not sure what she could have done differently. We had no respect for authority, parental or otherwise, and she had to work. We were just out of control.

Soccer and a Valuable Lesson

I played soccer throughout high school, a decent athlete and one of the leading scorers. I can't tell you how many games I played drunk and high, but it didn't seem to affect my performance. One day, though, I missed an important game. When I showed up for practice the next day, the soccer coach, Dan, taught me a valuable lesson about teamwork.

Coach told me to sit out for a while, and then he walked across the street to the White Hen Pantry. He bought a Score Bar and a Mountain Dew, came back across the street, and handed them to me, saying, "These are for you." Then he told the rest of the team to get on the line, and for the next fifteen minutes, he proceeded to run them like nobody's business. "This is the impact that you have on them," he said to me, "and you need to think about that. If you don't show up again, you are done." My relationship with the team changed after that. It was an amazing teaching moment, and I respected how Coach Avery handled it. The lesson he taught me stuck, and when I regained my senses, I internalized the importance of doing my job and the concept that the team and the mission come first.

Near-Death Experiences and a Stolen Trans Am

I was a sophomore in high school when I almost died from alcohol poisoning. I had gone to the home of my friend Derek and was drinking tons of beer and liquor. As always, it was a school day, and we were skipping. I was totally inebriated, but I decided to walk home, although Derek lived about ten miles from my house. I knew I was in real trouble when I dropped onto the field I was crossing and couldn't get up. A cop came by and asked me how much I had to drink, but I could not respond. He put me in the back of the car, and the last thing he said to me was, "Whatever you do, don't throw up in my car." I proceeded to vomit all over the seat, of course. He drove me to the hospital and called my parents. When they arrived, the ER staff were already pumping my stomach and suggested that my parents contact our local pastor. Fortunately, I recovered and was released from the hospital a day or two later.

The next time I nearly died involved drinking, drugs, and driving. A kid I had previously stolen a car with, John, had a souped-up Cutlass Supreme, and we were constantly bobbing around in it. One day, John was driving, a friend named Larry was in the right front seat, and I was in the back seat. By eight o'clock that morning—on a school day— we were already ridiculously drunk and had been smoking pot. We were on a two-lane highway without a barrier and realized that we were going way too fast as we drove over a hill coming to a stoplight. We couldn't see over the top of the hill, and Larry and I were screaming, "Pump the brakes! Pump the brakes!" John hit the brakes, and the car veered left into oncoming traffic, hitting an eighteen-wheeler head-on. The collision ripped the car in half, and the engine flew out and landed in someone's yard.

There was no way anyone should have survived. John broke his watch, and Larry broke his collarbone, but that was it for them. I went over the top of the backseat, my head hit the windshield, and I bounced back into the car. I had cuts all over my forehead and nose and remember looking down at my Levi jacket and seeing blood from my face pouring down all over it. The side windows had blown out, and— although the police had already arrived—I tried to throw all the beer cans out of the windows. One of the cops said, "*What* are you doing, dude?" Larry was pulled out with help from the "jaws of life," and off we went in the ambulance to the hospital. The picture of the car was big news in the local paper. That was my first experience with "bad press."

The dumbest thing I ever did was also the easiest thing. As I mentioned earlier, my friend John and I stole a car. We weren't car thieves, though; we were dope fiends who loved to do crazy things. We didn't know how to hijack a car, but back then, smaller used car dealerships usually had all their car keys laid out in a glass case with the car's name or year on the key. If you went into the dealership, took the car for a test ride, and were smart, you could leave with the key. We went to a dealership one Saturday, took the key, and returned when the dealership was closed on Sunday. Then we removed a license plate from one of the junk cars there and screwed it on the car we had chosen, a Trans Am. We had a great time driving it around for a while. Then it occurred to us that we would be charged with grand theft, so we hid the car in the woods. For a month, we kept sneaking back to our trophy to celebrate by partying and getting high.

Descent into Dealing

I was about fifteen and a sophomore in high school when I started to sell drugs. When you are a dope fiend, crime is inevitable, and for me, it began with theft. I had been stealing and running around like a crazy person since I was twelve. At fourteen or fifteen, I was in the school locker room, rifling through lockers and stealing any money I could find. Stealing a car from a car dealership with insurance left no marks on my conscience, but stealing twenty dollars from a kid, your dad, or your brother is very personal. Those are your relatives and friends, people who care about you. I would never have stolen from the soccer players on my team—I had some weird code of conduct around that—but anyone else in the locker room was fair game. Stealing from relatives and friends is one of my greatest sources of regret, creating a strong sense of shame to this day. If there is an upside, I never stole so much as a pencil after getting sober. Honesty and integrity became more than buzz words. Those who know me, including my own children, understand that I will do anything I can to help them, but if they lie to me or steal from me or others, they are on their own. Just tell me what happened, and we can work through it.

When soccer ended during my senior year, I lost all interest in school. I was fighting all the time, and in February of 1985, I was kicked out of school. Principal Flaherty said, "Man, you don't need to be here. You don't go to class, and there's no way you are going to graduate, so why don't we call it quits?" I was failing, causing problems, and a known drug dealer.

Drug Sales and Other Crimes

Once I left school, I moved out and signed a lease on an apartment with my roommate. He and I started selling drugs out of the apartment. My lifestyle as a drug dealer was both exciting and dreary. I started my day thinking, "What type of high do I want today? Do I want to do mushrooms? LSD? A combination of the two? Or is it going to be a big cocaine day?" The other side is the hustle of selling because you must pay for what you are consuming. At the peak, my consumption of cocaine alone was probably $250 to $300 a day—over $1,000 in today's currency. Rob and I sold inside and outside the apartment but tried to keep it outside because we lived in a residential neighborhood; constant foot and car traffic would stick out like a sore thumb.

Like any business, you have new sales, repeat sales, and collections, and collections are a critical piece. If we took delivery of a few thousand dollars' worth of drugs, the dealers would usually front the cost. In other words, if you have a relationship with a dealer, he gives you a line of credit. We would pay for what we had already received and then take a new delivery to use or sell, so we were always a payment behind. In other words, if you owed your dealer money, you had to have new sales and collect from users who owed you money.

I had two good friends who occasionally helped me collect. We would hop in the car and pop by the homes of a few delinquent customers. We even went to the homes of kids who lived with their parents, knocking on the door, and asking the parents if their son or daughter was around. Then we would go to another room with the kid and say, "Hey man, where's my f...... money?" Sometimes we didn't get paid. We might punch kids in the head, but more than likely, at the end of the day, we just threatened to stop doing business with them. That was a significant threat, especially if they had burned enough dealers in town and could no longer buy drugs there. In business, it's called freezing their line for lack of payment. It happened all the time.

While we were dealing, we continued to commit other crimes, and our arrest record grew. A couple of guys and I used to rob the same liquor warehouse all the time. First, we had to scale a fence, and then we had to pass through big, plastic, swinging louver doors that trucks would drive through all hours of the night to pick up their liquor orders. There was a massive selection of beer and liquor for us to choose from, and we would take whatever we could carry. The last time we did it, the police were waiting for us after we all climbed over the fence with our loot. It was late at night, and we took off running. I was cornered but kept trying to get away, infuriating the cops. Eventually, they caught me, threw me down, punched me several times, smacked me around, slapped on the handcuffs, and dragged me to a police car. I was arrested, thrown in jail again, and spent the night there. The police were super aggressive as they pressured me for the names of the two guys who had been with me, but I never gave them up. A misdemeanor is not worth risking any street cred.

I was also arrested for "breaking and entering" into a police station. My older brother had been at my apartment, and we had been partying. We decided to go for a ride in my brother's truck and were driving across a field when we saw the lights of a police car. We were caught and taken to the police station, where my brother, who was driving, was arrested. The rest of us had been riding in the truck bed and had no way home, so we were hanging outside the police station, still high as kites. Finally, I decided to climb up the front entrance of the police station to look in a window and see what was going on. The door had two short pillars on either side with a ledge above the entrance, so I climbed up one and walked over to the door's overhang underneath a window. I heard a shout, looked back, and there he was—a cop with a hand on his gun. Yikes. He was obviously not amused.

Christmas of 1985

1985 was the year I would have graduated from high school. It was also an example of how far I had descended into the life of a dope fiend. It was Christmas, and Rob, my roommate, was off somewhere, and i was home alone and high as a kite. I was spelling Merry Christmas with cocaine, snorting it all by myself. I had grown up in a close family that celebrated Christmas together, and my dad decided to stop by to wish me a Merry Christmas. When he looked at me, he cried. He stayed outside for a minute before heading home to celebrate with my mother and brothers. I preferred being alone and high. My drug use had become a sub-human existence in which the only thing that mattered was finding a way to get high.

Dad knew what was going on and would say things like, "You have that look in your eye today." But we never talked about it. I would only engage with my family when I got in trouble. I know they loved me, but they did not know how to deal with me. Years later, when I realized how much joy I had robbed from people, I felt terrible about it, but I was wholly absorbed in using and dealing in those days.

A couple of months later, in February 1986, the police raided my apartment. Neighbors had called them more than once because of the continual drug traffic, and they were aware of our activities. My dad was the publisher of the *Milford Daily News*, and one of his biggest competitors, the *Middlesex News*, ran the article of my arrest. They printed everything that the police confiscated, including drugs, cash, and drug paraphernalia, along with the names of everyone involved, describing Rob and me as "two major pushers of marijuana and cocaine in Framingham." That was my second experience with "bad press," one that hurt a lot of people. I was publicly known as a bad dude.

Me and my pit bull Grim visiting Mom and Dad after I moved out at 17

78 Summer St. in Framingham. Site of the final raid

4

REHAB AND A
DETERMINATION TO CHANGE

Court and My
Father's Advocacy

As I said before, the district attorney wanted to sentence me to ten years in Walpole, a state prison, which scared the s--- out of me. I would have only served a year as a first offender, but prison terrified me because some of the guys there were never getting out and were hard-core criminals. Worse yet, I knew some of the other dealers who were sentenced there. Not everybody on the street is your friend, and they would have been delighted to see me in prison. However, thanks to my father's relentless advocacy, I was given five years' probation and court-ordered to a substance abuse program, Spectrum House.

My father had no reason to believe that I was anything but a lost soul, but he went to every court date. He engineered a policy change to his company's insurance that covered mental health/substance abuse treatment so that I could get into a residential program. He never gave up trying to help, and I'll never forget that. The judge even said that I would have been sent to prison were it not for the family support.

Today, the relationship I have with my father was born out of his advocacy during that tough time. Before then, I didn't have much respect for his role as my father. We had even experienced physical altercations when I was a teenager. Then, when nobody should have, he stepped up, forming a lasting bond with me. Now I talk to him almost every day. We seek counsel from one another and solve family problems together. He is my best friend.

Detox

Before entering Spectrum House, I had to go through detox for three weeks, and the only detox was in Worcester State Hospital, a psychiatric hospital. My stay at the hospital was my first experience with crazy people in a confined situation versus crazy people on the street. I was in a ward designed for heroin addicts and slept in a room with eight to ten other guys. The heavy heroin users were given methadone but were still what we called "dope sick" and would walk around with wet towels on their necks and heads, constantly patting their faces. They were also angry, especially shortly before their next methadone dose, and they would harass or threaten others in the ward. After the dose, the ward calmed down, and everyone could breathe again.

I was a little 145-pound strung-out white guy, but two men there, Lou and Alex, befriended and protected me. Lou and Alex were friends, ex-cons who had known each other before they came into detox. Alex slept in the bed across from me. Alex was a fun-loving guy, just a hustler, and we played a lot of ping-pong together. Lou was a big, muscular, fierce-looking man who, if you had a problem, would take care of it—even if that meant shooting somebody. He and Alex helped me when I had a problem with an older guy in the bed next to Alex, who was constantly harassing me. A large, physically fit guy in his mid-30s, that man hated everyone. Late one night, when he was probably dope sick, he started to bully me. Alex told him to leave me alone, but the guy kept on, and then he began to walk towards my bed. I don't remember what I had said to set him off, but I knew he could kill me and had never been so scared in my life. Alex, whose leg was hobbled by a boot, got up in the guy's face and said, "I told you to leave the kid alone," and then Lou said, "Everybody, go to bed," and that was it. I would see Lou and Alex again at Spectrum House, where we were close for a while, and they treated me well. Two hardened criminals were kind to me, and I learned that no one is ever all good or all bad. Of course, the first thing they did when I got there was take my Marlboro cigarettes. Like I always say, you take the good with the bad, and you can't love half of a person. I was grateful for their help and happy to part with the butts.

Spectrum House

I have been in some bizarre situations, but nothing compares to what I experienced at Spectrum House. Every new resident gets assigned to the service crew, where you clean the same bathrooms with a cloth and toothbrush— all day, every day. After dinner, we went to extremely confrontational counseling groups where people would scream at each other at the top of their lungs. Spectrum House would have house cleaning guilt sessions every couple of months, entire days when people would "cop" to their guilt. For example, someone would stand up and say, "On my last court visit, Pat and I went to my house. I got drunk, and I had sex with my wife." Sex was considered a privilege and required applying for permission. Since the driver (Pat) was implicated, he had to stand up and admit it. The severity of punishments depended on whether you implicated yourself or someone else implicated you. It was a chess game that would go on for hours. Should I admit my "guilt" (rules broken) or stay quiet and hope my name doesn't come up again in someone else's guilt? As I look back, this feels like the 1980s version of our modern-day Congress.

Spare Parts

The worst punishment was referred to as spare parts. If that happened, everyone shunned you for up to a week, and you were forbidden to look anyone in the eye. You also walked around with a toothbrush, constantly scrubbing floors, and even ate facing a wall kitty-corner during meals. Other punishments included wearing a sign around your neck explaining what you did, and every time you entered a room, you had to read the sign out loud. So, for example, if you ate things you weren't supposed to eat, your sign might say, "Because I cannot control my feelings, I cover my feelings with food." The year I was there, spare parts was the one punishment consistently causing residents to quit. They figured, how is jail any worse?

The purpose of the punishments was to break you down as a human. If someone told a staff person you had broken a rule, you would get what was called a knock. You were sent to a room, knocked on the door, and entered it to find a staff person and two senior residents waiting for you. Next, you stood in the middle of that room while each person screamed at you for five minutes, calling you every nasty name in the book. There was one response allowed after each person was through screaming, and that was, "Thank you. I learned a lot." But when you left the room, you felt like killing someone.

The program involved more than punishment, though, and I had some good times, too. I made a few friends and read a lot of good books. I also learned some valuable skills from some of my assignments.

Kitchen Crew and the Potato Heist

After service crew, I was assigned full-time to "pan," which meant kitchen work. I learned how to cook, take care of a kitchen, make soup from scratch, and cook with a roux. I eventually became head of the kitchen crew. I took my role seriously, and in my desire to be a hero, I made my last and final heist; I stole a box of beautiful, fresh baking potatoes. Just like before, it didn't end well for me.

Every Thursday, the kitchen crew would get up at three in the morning to drive an hour to the Chelsea produce markets, where trucks would deliver vegetables, flowers, and all forms of produce. I would go to each vendor and say, "Hi, my name is Tim, and I'm from Spectrum House. Do you have any donations for us today?" They usually gave us a smashed box or two of potatoes, 80% good and twenty percent bad. On the week of Thanksgiving, I couldn't resist; I stole a *beautiful* box of potatoes, and another resident saw me do it. It was one of those the ends justifies the means moments. The theft eventually came out in the next house cleaning episode, and I was stuck in the kitchen for a week scrubbing the same shelves and floors with iodine all day. In that case, the punishment was worth the crime.

Ticket Teams

One of my first lessons in sales came from selling raffle tickets on the Spectrum House ticket teams. Staff members drove four or five teams of two people to local grocery stores, where the ticket teams would stand outside at the exit or the entrance. They would identify themselves as residents at Spectrum House, explaining that it was a drug and alcohol rehabilitation center. Then they would say, "Would you like to buy a raffle ticket?" That was the beginning of my education in sales. I learned that if you tell someone, "They're a dollar a piece or six for five bucks," they would only buy one. But if you tell someone, "They are twelve for ten dollars, but I know you would never buy all twelve, so I can give you six for five dollars," they would buy six for five dollars. In other words, if I changed the value proposition, I could increase my revenue. The team kept it interesting by challenging each other to see who could sell the most tickets with a prize like a pack of cigarettes and a soda, luxury items for us. The competition was fierce, but I became an excellent sales guy and would tear through 40 books of tickets by about two o'clock. We weren't picked up until five o'clock, so I sat there with a Diet Coke and a pack of cigarettes, waiting. As I mentioned in the introduction, I discovered I was naturally gifted at two things—selling and teaching people how to sell. Those were important data points in my career exploration, although I didn't realize it at the time. For the younger folks, if you think you might be good at something and consider that as a career, give it a try first in a real-world setting. Doing so will save you lots of wasted time later in life.

Sadly, many of the people on ticket teams never returned to the house; they just took the money and left the program. These were people you were close to, but you never knew if or when they would leave. Almost 100% of the people in the program were court-ordered there, and many went back to jail when they left. Most were heroin addicts and could not stay away from it despite going through detox and then Spectrum House.

My Decision to Change

The program was brutal, but my fear of being hurt in prison, along with my experiences at Spectrum House, motivated me to finish and choose a different way of life. *And it is a choice!*

I met a woman named Valerie while at Spectrum House. Valerie was the person who had the most significant impact on me, at least in terms of her kindness and support. A Black sex worker and heroin addict, Valerie spent every cigarette break with me, and we took long walks during the few months we were together. She was an easy person to be with and was very maternal towards me. Valerie was in her mid-to-late-30s with two children, and I was only twenty years old and not close to my mother at the time. Valerie had repeatedly lost then regained her children to DCYF because of her substance abuse and had been in and out of jail. She would say, "Hey, I chose this life. You are still young and have so much potential. Don't do what I did." Valerie convinced me to get my GED while in rehab and move away from my previous bad habits and behavior. I was young and naively hoped that Valerie would change, but she walked away from a ticket team one day and never returned. That was my worst day at Spectrum House; I was devastated. But Valerie left me even more determined to change my life.

Before my arrest, Rob, my roommate and partner in crime, was another reason I was afraid to continue my former lifestyle. After our arrest, while I was in rehab, he was arrested two more times and sent to prison. Once I knew he was in prison, I could visualize myself in the same situation if I continued down the path he had chosen.

My observations of Valerie's life, Rob's incarceration, and the lives of other hard-core addicts or criminals contributed to my decision to change. I saw older men with knife scars on their bellies and overheard a Hispanic man sharing a story about pouring gasoline on a kid and setting him on fire. Even before I heard his story, I was afraid of the man because he had a dark presence about him. My fears intensified as I listened to his story, and it was one of those defining moments when I felt like I was in the wrong universe and had to get out. I realized that if I did not change, I could be back in Spectrum House 30 years later or end up in prison or dead. I lived with real criminals doing real crime before I went to rehab and realized that I meant nothing to anyone in the drug world.

So, I obtained my GED in 1987 and left Spectrum House that spring, determined to change. Thanks to my dad, I had a job waiting for me and took the first step into my new life.

PART TWO

BEGINNING THE ROAD TO SUCCESS

"The best part is still ahead of me—I haven't experienced my 'good old days' yet." —Luther Vandros

5

COLLEGE YEARS
AND STREET SMARTS

Transitioning from Rehab

I get asked the following question all the time: "How did you go from where you were to where you are now?" I respond the same way every time:

I take full responsibility for what I did. I do not blame anyone for anything. They were MY choices, and I own them. Personal accountability is the most liberating feeling in the world. Why? Once you realize YOU alone are responsible for your life, you know you can overcome almost any obstacle. However, if you stay tethered to the past by blaming others, you can never move beyond the feeling of helplessness.

One of my favorite quotes is, "If it is to be, it is up to me" (William Johnsen). My life until I left rehab was out of control, and I made a pact that I was *never* going back. I hated being broke and letting people down, and I *really* hated giving people control of my life due to bad decision-making. Finally, I was ready to leave the past behind and create a new way of living, and when I left Spectrum House, my dad helped me take the first step—an honest job.

My dad had a job for me when I left Spectrum House. He put me to work in the circulation department of his newspaper, where I delivered bundles to local carriers and worked on the assembly line getting bundles to the commercial drivers. I became a whiz at doing math in my head because I had to stack the papers according to the number needed by an individual carrier's paper route. In real-time, stacks came down in bundles of 25. So, a route with 37 papers meant 25 plus twelve, which left thirteen for the next bundle. On and on I went until bundles for all the routes were filled. To this day, I rarely meet someone who can do basic math and percentages in their head faster than me, and I attribute that to my time with the press assembly line—again, real-world experience. Unfortunately, Dad was a bigger man than me, as I would have fired myself after I crashed two vans while delivering papers to the carriers. But, again, that is the personification of loving the whole person.

One of the high school students working at the newspaper, Nicole, influenced my decision to apply for college. Nicole and I began to date, and we had fun going to her senior prom, something I had missed out on. I attended without using alcohol or cocaine and truly enjoyed myself. As we became closer, I got to know Nicole's friends and heard their discussions about college and what they wanted to do with their lives, subjects I had not thought about until then. Being around that group of people inspired me, so I went to my dad and said, "Hey, I think I want to go to college." He replied, "That's awesome!" and said he would reach out to one of his acquaintances at Dean Junior College, a two-year community college not far from our home.

At the same time, I called the soccer coach at Dean, a good guy, and told him I was thinking about going there. I also told him about my past and was honest about everything. He was sympathetic and said, "I play on a men's team in Wrentham, where Dean is located, so why don't you come down and play with us?" After three or four weeks of playing on that team and getting to know him, he said, "I would love for you to be on the college team and will help you in any way I can."

My dad and the coach came with me on my admissions interview with no high school transcripts, armed only with my GED. The coach said he had gotten to know me and that I was a solid soccer player who could contribute to the college team. The admissions person said, "OK, here is what we're going to do. You will take one course this summer and earn a B or better, and then we will admit you." Then he said, "Welcome to Dean." My dad broke down in tears, and the coach was all fired up. I took a psychology class, earned an A, and began my freshman year in the fall of 1987.

That was my first big boy win, and I learned two valuable lessons that I would apply over and over again:

1. What do I have to trade with actual or perceived value, and how can I use it to get what I want?
2. Win the crowd, and you will win your freedom. Remember the movie *Gladiator* and the day Russell Crowe discovers that winning the crowd was the key to winning his freedom? In the case of Dean, my soccer coach represented the crowd, and I was on my way to professional freedom.

Dean Junior College

When I arrived at Dean Junior College, I went to work. In addition to playing soccer, I joined every club imaginable, maintained a 3.5 GPA, and worked part-time selling advertising for my dad's newspaper. Before graduating from Dean, I had earned an academic scholarship for my second year. In addition, I received the prestigious Fletcher Prize, awarded by the college president to one man and one woman each year. During my second year, I also became an RA, a resident assistant, which allowed me to live on campus for free.

I had some challenging experiences as an RA at Dean and later as an RA when I attended Bryant College. In both situations, my age and the street smarts I had gained during my drug-dealing days came in handy.

The craziest experiences I had at Dean always involved the football team. Dean had a decent football team, but the players thought none of the campus rules applied to them. Dean was a dry campus, but that didn't stop anyone from drinking. When I made rounds in the dorm, I could see the bottles, but I had a simple rule: Keep your door shut and put a towel under it if you are smoking pot. I was the most liberal RA in the world. But we all have a breaking point.

One day a big kid walked out of his room, reeking of pot and with a colossal joint stuck in his ear. I said, "Hey, bro, what are you doing?" and flicked the joint out of his ear. He pushed me, and his buddies came out and gave me a hard time. I thought things would get physical but was able to deescalate the situation. Stuff like that happened all the time.

The saddest incident I dealt with involved suicide. One of the guys who lived on my floor had real emotional issues, always drunk and acting stupid, and sometimes he would end up crying on the floor. I would bring him to my room and talk to him. He threatened to kill himself for months, but we did not take it seriously until it happened. Finally, one night he drove down the street to a warehouse in Franklin, where he ran a hose from the exhaust to the window and killed himself. I was asked to speak with his parents, and I will never forget the pain on his dad's face. It hit me like a ton of bricks. My own parents had been dealing with my insanity for years, and I can't imagine the number of times they were worried that I would not survive. I deeply regret that.

Bryant University Years

After graduating from Dean Junior College, I attended Bryant College, now Bryant University. This time I had a real sense of purpose. The routine became easier as I grew more accustomed to college life in and out of the classroom, but I still had a rebellious streak, and the two beasts were starting to feud again.

Because I was a transfer student, I didn't know anyone and was assigned to a suite with a 350-pound guy who had the worst congestion problems in the world and terrible body odor. It was awful. We were juniors, and in our suite were three freshmen, another group of juniors, and the RA, who was involved in everything on campus.

I had started drinking again at that point. You could only drink in your room if you were 21, which by then I was, and only if there were no freshmen in your suite. I was not following that rule; my friend Don and I always had people over in the suite and drinking, and the RA and I were at constant odds with each other. I was still a bit rebellious inside and was "written up" for not following dorm rules. Not following dorm rules seemed trivial given my past, but it was not without consequences: I had to meet with the head of residence life. After talking with me for a while, she framed the conversation as a power struggle between myself and my suitemate, the RA. She asked me as a favor to tone it down. And then something amazing happened;

she told me there was an opening for an RA position in a fraternity dorm and asked if I was interested. She thought I had the perfect experience and personality to keep things under control. To the best of my knowledge, I was the only resident in Bryant's history to be put on housing probation and offered a job as an RA, all in the span of 30 minutes. Score one assist for the bad beast!

Bryant did not have Greek housing, but it was a Greek-run campus with two all-fraternity dorms. Each floor would house a different fraternity. At Bryant, students had to apply for a party permit, which meant they could have 50 people in the suites. There were frequent parties and managing them was very difficult. I only had one rule: if they had a party, someone there had to be sober enough for me to talk to them. I always enjoyed it, though. I managed to find a way to stay in the chaos. It was part of my street-side; I liked the adrenaline rush—and I was also able to use it to reason with some pretty big personalities. I used a combination of logic and leverage. When I spoke with them, they understood that we would have a problem if they didn't take me seriously. Some of the greatest negotiations I have ever had took place on campus under some tough circumstances. My ability to negotiate, combined with managing chaos under challenging circumstances, would serve me well as I progressed in my professional life.

Bonnie

Meeting Bonnie and Greek Life

Bonnie and I were in the same sociology class and often hung out with friends at the Country Comfort, the campus bar. I lived in the dorm right across the street from the Comfort. One night, as we were all pouring out of the bar with her friends, I ran up to her, acting crazy and showing off in front of my roommates. I picked her up, carried her to my dorm, and tried to convince her to come upstairs to my room. She would have nothing to do with it. She asked me to put her down and said, "Why don't we do this instead? I'll see you tomorrow morning in class, and if you remember me and my name, we can have a conversation." I was pumped up. To make sure I got a second chance, my roommates put a sticky note on the door of my suite saying, her name is Bonnie!

The next day, after asking one of her friends in class, "Which one is Bonnie?" I stopped her as she left class. After a few shy and awkward moments, we began to spend time together. It wasn't long before we were spending every free moment together.

Bonnie was the president of her sorority her junior year and took the local chapter nationally. She was very active in the Greek community, and I took a lot of flak from the Greeks because I was not in a fraternity. It almost felt like a racist situation, dating outside of the community. They would tell me I was never going to get anywhere with her. I refused to join a fraternity because I saw how the guys treated each other, especially the hazing. The irony of that is all my kids are in Greek life. My oldest son was the social director of his fraternity, and my daughter was the vice president and treasurer of a sorority. My youngest son is currently in a fraternity. Bonnie loved Greek life, and I realize it has a lot of benefits, but it was never a good fit for me.

The first time Bonnie and I spent apart was spring break in March 1991. She went to the Bahamas, and I went to Fort Lauderdale, where the strangest thing happened. As my roommates and I were hanging out on the beach, we were approached by a camera crew filming B-roll footage for a popular HBO series. They asked us a few questions about sex, had us sign a waiver, and off they went. I thought nothing of it until years later when I worked at the bank in telemarketing, and the bank's VP coyly asked me if I had gone to Fort Lauderdale for spring break that year. Puzzled, I said yes. Grinning, he told me he was flipping channels the night before and happened to catch me on HBO being interviewed on the controversial show *Real Sex*. My interview was less than a minute on a one-hour show, so he was obviously not flipping channels. *Real Sex* was essentially a soft porn show. Gotcha, buddy! I was out of telemarketing within a week, but we would go on to become friends and would joke about that first encounter for years. It was also an interesting conversation for Bonnie and me years later. Score a second assist for the bad beast!

After spring break, Bonnie and I became inseparable. We were both marketing majors, and our last names began with an "S," so we had the experience of walking together hand in hand at our graduation. We also couldn't have had more polar opposite upbringings and life experiences, and I feel like that was a big part of the attraction for both of us. We graduated in May 1991, and I proposed that summer. We married a year later, in August 1992. Twenty-nine years and three kids later, selling her is still the greatest deal I have ever put together.

The Disclosure

While I was dating Bonnie, one of the kids from my hometown told some people that I was a drug dealer. Then one day, Bonnie said she had heard something about me and wanted to talk. So we went for a ride, and she asked me if I was a drug dealer. I told her the truth. I said, "I was a drug dealer, a convicted felon currently on a two-and-a-half-year suspended sentence and probation for five years as we speak. I've done many bad things, and that is who I used to be. That's not who I am now, and I'm never going back to that." I don't remember Bonnie's exact words, but she replied that my explanation made sense and my past didn't bother her. She added that she was proud of me and congratulated me for having the courage to change my life. That's who Bonnie is at the core—one of the least judgmental people I have ever met.

Bonnie and I have always had an intense relationship, and I suspect a part of her enjoyed an occasional adrenaline rush as well, liking the idea of being with a "bad boy." She has often stated that what happened in the past has nothing to do with the present or the future. Once again, I didn't realize it at the time, but she was the perfect wife and partner for a risk-taking business guy.

We didn't tell Bonnie's parents about my past until a few years ago because we weren't sure how they would react to it. Bonnie thought it best to keep my past to herself. She said she was going to marry me either way, so why rock the boat. When we finally told them, they thought we were joking. Her mother was in denial at first, saying, "No, that's not true." Her father just walked away. They are lovely, wonderful people, but they are normal humans with little exposure to folks with my background. But family is also the most important thing to them, and it never changed their opinion of the man they believed their daughter had married. We are very close and spend lots of time together.

Our Contract

Early in our marriage, Bonnie and I made a critically important decision. We began to have children and were starting to juggle work and childcare. I said, "We can both work and share all responsibilities, or we can set up a contract that says, 'Bonnie will take care of all things domestic, and Tim will take care of all things financial.'" We did not literally write a contract but were in 100% agreement. Bonnie wanted to be home with our children. I wanted to work without receiving calls about children who fell and scraped their knees during the day.

My wife had the same degree as I had, and it could be argued that she was more accomplished in college. She was president of her sorority, active in the school community, and had a good job as soon as she graduated. But her priority was being a full-time mother, a vital part of her identity. Quite frankly, she did the most demanding work through the years, and it shows in her close relationships with our children. I am also close to them, but she has always been far more compassionate and emotionally available. Our contract would become the most important decision of our life together.

Bonnie and I at Bryant College graduation

Marrying my beautiful bride

Dean Junior College commencement day

Nervously powering through the announcement of the class gift

Receiving the Fletcher Prize from Dean President

**DEAN CAPTAIN — Tim
Sawyer of Mendon was a captain on Dean Junior College's
soccer team this fall. Sawyer is
on the Dean's list and a member of the Phi Theta Kappa
National Honor Society.**

Newspaper photo from Dean soccer team

First job working for my Dad at the Milford Daily News

6

FIRST AND LAST W-2 JOB

Bonnie and I graduated from Bryant College in 1991 with BAs in marketing and business administration. Right after she graduated, Bonnie was hired as an underwriter for an insurance company with a good starting salary. I interviewed for a job at a bank but did not hear back from them immediately. I had worked for my dad throughout college, and he promoted me to marketing director at the newspaper, giving me a raise that matched Bonnie's salary. He believed that we should be equally yoked as best we could, including our incomes. It was a bit of a stretch for the smaller newspaper, but that's who my dad is.

A month or so after my promotion, I received a call from the bank. They offered to start me in their training program as a telemarketer selling mortgages and to pay me $10,000 per year plus commission. My dad thought I should take it because of the growth potential, so I accepted the position. It was my first "real W-2 job," aside from the one with my father, and for over ten years, it was the perfect training ground for my future endeavors as an entrepreneur.

Working for a Subprime Mortgage Lender

The bank was the poster child for subprime mortgages. The business model involved buying as much information about the consumer as possible, targeting potential borrowers with fair to poor FICO scores who had missed a mortgage payment, were late on a car payment, or had 80% of their credit utilized. The bank used direct mail to encourage people to consolidate their bills, and it advertised a very low-interest rate. My first job, as a telemarketer, involved taking customer calls and obtaining a complete application, including their social security number. Next, the bank would complete a credit check and underwrite the loan based on the information provided on the application. Upon approval, the borrower would receive a conditional loan proposal, subject to verifying their income, credit, and equity in their home. The process was tricky as many of these factors changed during the loan process. Next, the telemarketer/salesperson would explain the reason for the loan's interest rate and fee structure—why it was different from the advertised rate in the mailing—and then he would begin the process of justifying the cost. That was the psychology of the sale, and I loved it. I was young, still relatively naive, and for the most part, I believed we were helping people by lowering their monthly payments and consolidating high-interest credit cards. At the time, I rarely thought about the ethics of what we were doing. I had discovered I was great at it; it was legal, and I was motivated by the ability to make more money. The borrowers had bankruptcies, credit problems, and other difficult financial circumstances. That meant increased risk to the bank and hence, a higher cost of borrowing. I thought we were doing these folks a favor and loved the challenge of helping them to see the logic in it. That's not to say I was not tempting the bad beast in me, and like clockwork, he was right on time.

I remember I tried to do a loan for a divorced man who had custody of his kids, but he had a lien on his house from his ex-wife. I told him there was no way we could do the loan because of the lien on the title and said, "How much time do you spend with the kids versus how much time she spends?" Finally, I convinced him to allow me to call his ex-wife and offer her custody if she would take the lien off the house. I would have made $1,200 if she had agreed, but when I called, she went postal. She said, "What kind of human being would contact me at work to suggest that?" Well, ma'am, the kind of man who is blinded by getting ahead and is willing to do what is necessary to make that happen.

As one of my managers said, I took to selling like a duck to water. I became the guy to call on any closing in the country that was going wrong. The managers would allow me to tap into anyone's phone at any time, and I would successfully guide the loan officers and customers through the negotiation process. For me, it was like playing a game, and I was a great gamer. I was caught up in the game and wanted to be the best subprime mortgage guy ever.

From Telemarketer to Origination Manager

I was a fast learner, and after three months in telemarketing, I was promoted to a loan officer position. Within a year, I became a top producer. By the second year, I was number one out of 30 and held that spot until I was promoted to origination manager three years later, and my pay more than tripled. After my promotion to manager, I lost a lot of friends. At the time, a good loan officer could make $65,000. An origination manager could make $150k plus. Promotions were few and far between, and the idea that one of them could have taken my spot if they had stayed later, worked harder, or produced more, was a lot to process. I learned a valuable life lesson that I have shared in talks for years: *There is a cumulative effect of your life's decisions*. It's not what happened the day before an event; it's about what you did in the years leading up to it.

Mr. Big Shot

My first obstacle was a horrible manager named J. His claim to fame was playing football in college and being written up in *Sports Illustrated* as an unsung hero. J was mean to everyone, especially the salespeople. One day, the young man sitting next to me, who had diabetes, asked J for a break so he could check his blood sugar levels. J said, "You haven't sold anything today, so why don't you wait until you get a sale?" When one of the guys sitting behind me stood up and said, "J, leave the kid alone and let him do his thing," J stood up, and the chairs went flying. Of course, some of us stayed on the phone during the melee. We had quotas to hit.

J was even mean to me, although I made him more money than anyone else. I'll never forget the day he was furious about some of the loans I had made. As part of processing any mortgage with a current lien on the home, I was required to obtain a payoff from the existing lender. Back then, banks did not cooperate as they do now. They would delay giving you the payoff amount, call the customer, and say, "What are they offering you? We can do better," and with the more competitive lenders, this would occasionally end up blowing your deal. So, instead of calling for the payoff, I could determine the balance through the credit bureau, current mortgage statement, and a copy of the note. X-factors were the last payment made, the next payment due, or if there was a prepayment penalty. I had a few loans close under this scenario, and the payoffs were short. That meant an adjustment would have to be made to the borrower's proceeds. That was not a bank-condoned practice. However, the consequence of a short payoff would be far less than the consequences associated with losing a loan to a competing lender. It was one of those "pick your poison" deals. So, Mr. Big Shot took me into the basement of the building carrying four huge, green folders under his arms. These were the short payoff files. He screamed at me like no one's business, took all four folders and threw them at me, scattering papers everywhere. The bank owner would have said, "Timmy, be more careful. I understand why you didn't call for the payoffs." It would have been better to anger a customer than to lose the deal altogether, and he understood that.

My wife, Bonnie, was frustrated and could not understand why I put up with J's behavior. One incident, in particular, sent her frustration level over the top. My friend and fellow loan officer, Mike, was getting married about an hour's drive from the bank, and the ceremony was due to start at one o'clock on a Saturday. We worked most Saturdays, although they weren't very productive, and I asked Mr. Big Shot if I could come to the bank in my suit and leave an hour early to get to the ceremony on time. Even though I was the top producer, he said, "We'll see how it goes." Sure enough, that Saturday, when I asked if I could leave, J said he just couldn't do it. He said, "Let's try to get one more before you leave." I missed almost the entire ceremony, and Bonnie was in shock. So, I explained my thinking about it to her. For starters, I was a convicted felon with a recent criminal record making good money working for a bank. Secondly, having people like J in power at the bank was not necessarily bad because a younger, more driven employee could replace an insecure, somewhat incompetent manager. What Bonnie saw as cruelty, I saw as an opportunity, and within two years, I was promoted to J's position.

My impression of most corporate environments is that the primary goal is to get ahead by shifting blame while keeping other folks down. I never understood that. I always felt the better approach is to focus on developing team members, helping them get what they want from their career, and in turn, we would all do better as a result. It turns out, based on my track record managing teams, I was 100% right. So much for Mr. Big Shot.

Employee Resistance to Training

Another obstacle was the resistance I faced from other loan officers when it came to my ideas for training. As a loan officer, my colleagues on the other teams often came to me for help with their deals. I would happily hop on the call with their customers to overcome objections and get the deal back on track. I loved training and knew I was good at it. All the loan officers knew if there was a problem, transfer them to 447, my extension. At the time, there was no formal sales training; no guides or manuals had ever been created for a uniform approach to selling. I started by making a list of the most frequently asked questions and the most common objections from potential borrowers. I shared my "training document" with the president and owner of the bank. I also offered to train the team as a group. The other loan officers disliked the idea, asking me why I wanted to rock the boat and accused me of brown-nosing, but the big guy loved it, and we set a date for our first official scripted corporate training.

Before that happened, I had to deal with a significant problem: my uncontrollable fear of public speaking. I could outsell anyone over the phone but doing that in front of people almost paralyzed me. Nevertheless, I practiced, ran many miles to burn adrenaline, and powered through the training. The content was excellent, but I was a nervous wreck, and everyone could tell from the sweat stains under my arms to the perspiration on my forehead. It was brutal. After the event, I was waiting for expected criticism from the big guy, but all he said was, "Well, that was kind of rough, but you did well. I think we should do it again." He may not have realized it at the time, but that one act of kindness, that one statement of encouragement, changed my life.

Overcoming a Fear of Public Speaking

I realized that I had to conquer my fear of public speaking in order to advance my career, so I sought professional help. I visited a psychiatrist who explained that I was caught in a loop; as soon as I thought about speaking, I would immediately experience intense anxiety. He prescribed medication to take each time it happened, and I eventually learned to control the physiological reaction. I still take medication occasionally and sometimes experience anxiety before speaking, but I began to love public speaking and soon became a corporate trainer and recruiter.

My experience with public speaking became a mantra for me through the years: "That which you fear most, once tamed, will become your greatest asset." Thirty years later, public speaking is like oxygen for me.

Becoming a Corporate Recruiter and Trainer

At the bank, the loan officer's primary function was to help the borrower understand that what we were offering made the most sense given their circumstances, and I wanted to teach loan officers how to do that. Based on my track record of success closing deals, I felt like I understood the process better than most. It was never about the rate or the fees. It came down to a human connection and a sense of trust. Unsolicited, I set to the task of writing a sales manual. By the time I completed it, the manual was around 80 pages long and contained everything a loan officer needed to deal with the modern subprime borrower. This thing was legit. I worked until 8:30 p.m. most evenings, and after some time with Bonnie and the kids, I worked on the manual at home. I could not write it at work because we weren't allowed to have computers on our desks (nor were we allowed to use email—this was 1997); we had some real upper management control issues at that place, thermostats included.

Once we started to use the manual, I realized the best salespeople were those right out of college with little to no real-world job experience—just like me. Recruiting was as much about the parents as it was about the graduate. So, we revamped the compensation plan to make it more attractive. Instead of offering a base pay of only $10,000 a year plus commission—while knowing the average person would make $45,000—we guaranteed parents that their son or daughter would never earn less than $800 a week. The base pay remained $10,000, but we created a specific draw structure. They would get the $800 a week, but they might end the month with a deficit if their base plus commissions didn't exceed that amount. At the end of the year, the bank would either fire them or wipe out their deficit and allow them to start over. At the time, $42,000 was a decent salary for a recent graduate. The net result was that we ended up with higher-quality candidates without increasing our aggregate payroll costs.

After I wrote the manual, I began a recruitment program to hire only college students, doing the recruiting myself. Every year, I traveled to five different campuses and cultivated excellent relationships with the career placement folks. As a result, we had our pick of the best candidates. Once recruited and hired, the new employees had to go through the manual and a comprehensive training course before touching a phone, and we would role play with an actual unconnected phone. The training added a lot of sophistication to the bank's sales approach because we were teaching the psychology behind it. The training program also created uniformity by ensuring that everyone followed the steps that offered the highest probability of success.

During this process, I came to love teaching, and seeing new loan officers thrive in our system became my number one passion. The joy of successful teaching would stay with me for the rest of my professional career. I have taught tens of thousands of salespeople, small business owners, and elective medical folks. The funny thing is, the process is essentially the same, regardless of the trinket, widget, or gadget you are trying to sell.

Disillusionment and Betrayal

Working for the bank, aka subprime mortgage company, meant working for a sales organization, so I thrived there, and the money translated into a more comfortable life for my family. In addition to increased earning potential, the bank held sales contests every year, so I would bust my butt to make sure I won. I would always finish first or second, and this would allow us to go on great vacations at no cost. Aside from going to Disney World with my family in fourth grade, I didn't get the chance to travel much growing up, so I was really motivated to win—not to mention my hero complex. The idea of going home and telling Bonnie I didn't win just wasn't an option for me.

As my work situation improved, Bonnie eventually quit her job to stay at home with our children, and we bought a new house in an upscale neighborhood with what I thought at the time was a big mortgage. I borrowed $240k on a house we bought for $297k. For me, that was a big stretch mentally and all the motivation I needed to get going.

While there were excellent economic benefits working for the bank, the schedule was crazy and took much of my time and energy. I had developed a routine of working at the bank for 50 hours a week minimum, including Saturdays; everything in my life had taken a back seat to my career. I had given up control of my life by creating a costly lifestyle, and I began to resent it. Towards the end of my job at the bank, it became less satisfying.

Employer vs. Employee Relationships

I was confident that the big guy and I would work together forever, even though he was in his 60s and I was in my 30s. Most of the business lessons I ever learned were from him, such as "success is a numbers game," "there is no easy way to make money," and "work comes first." The big guy had an interesting perspective on life. He was a tough, ruthless businessperson who would do whatever it took to get where he wanted to go. At the same time, next to Adam DeGraide, he was the most generous person I had ever met regarding philanthropy. I'm talking about giving away millions. As I look back on it, he had this Robin Hood thing going where you did what you had to do to help the people and the organizations you cared about. Period. If I had to trust my professional career to anyone, it would have been him. But sadly, our relationship would change. I saw him as a father figure and a friend, but in the end, he would see me as an employee, not as a son.

I always advocated for new pay plans, incentives, and competitions for the sales team because I believed incentives made sense in motivating them. Maybe I was projecting my own value system, but it worked. One day while I was discussing this with the bank's CEO, he said, "Tim, you fail to grasp the role of the employer versus the role of the employee. The employee's role is to get as much money as possible for the least amount of work. The employer's role is to get as much work out of the employee as possible for the least amount of money." I thought that was a terrible, jaded, and shortsighted attitude, but that was his mantra and that of the company. I wanted to say, "I'm right here, buddy. I'm the employee, the guy you're trying to get the most from. Come on, motivate *me*."

The other really strange part about being a manager was the idea that we received 80% of our pay in one check at the end of the year. There were no contracts, guarantees, or written formulas regarding the amount. It was bizarre; we just had to have blind faith that they would do the right thing. So, on Christmas Eve, I would get a check that could be anywhere from $80,000 to $150,000, but I had no idea what it was going to be. The vice-president would walk around and tease everyone, saying, "Oh, well, the big guy's not here today, so you might not get your checks." It was like a massive head game, and it was tough if you did not have the mental constitution to deal with it. It taught me what not to do when I was responsible for motivating my own sales teams.

The End of a Promising Career

The big guy treated me almost like a son. He would come to sit at my cube for long periods to talk about business and family, and he always had a couple of great stories. I loved this guy and would do whatever he asked me to do. He occasionally gave me his credit card and told me to take Bonnie away for the weekend, saying, "It's on me." You can't imagine how good that felt for someone with my background. He made me feel like I had self-worth, until our relationship became an issue for one of his sons, which ultimately led to my termination after twelve years.

The big guy had four sons, all of whom worked at the bank at some point. One of them did not appreciate the time I spent with his dad. I understood and realized this would not end well despite reassurances that it was all in my head. The big guy would openly talk about how he and I were different: "We're street guys, salespeople, motivators." It was true but not helpful in terms of my co-existence with his kids. Eventually, one of his sons began to threaten my role at the bank, saying things like, "Your job is going to change. There will be no more managing other loan officers, and everyone is going to have the same job with the same pay." This kid was a terrible public speaker who was very uncomfortable addressing the team at company meetings. His father encouraged him to speak, but he would lean against a wall and look down at his shoes. I would get up, put my arm around him, and say, "I think what he is trying to say is … ," and I would give the speech while he stood next to me. It was emasculating for him, and he eventually took it out on me.

The relationship between him and I became so bad that he told his father he could not sleep at night knowing I worked there. "It is him or me," he said. Attempts to work things out between us failed, and when I let the big guy know that his son and I could not co-exist in the same bank, we both teared up. It was very emotional. For almost thirteen years, I had often worked twelve hours a day and every Saturday treating every dime lent as if it were my own money. But in the end, it all came down to one thing: I did not own the place, and I was an employee at will. I was 33, and my career had been blown up by an angry little kid who, with zero experience, happened to be the bank's new president. Needless to say, that was a lesson I will not soon forget.

I had just lost a job making $250k per year with a wife and three children at home. I had no plan or prospects, and I had a criminal record. But my wife's reaction when I told her I lost my job reminded me of how lucky I was to have married her. It was on a Monday, and when I returned home around noon, she was out. I called her from home and told her I had left the bank and had no plan to return. All she said was, "Good for you. You don't need that s--- in your life every day. I'm sure you will figure it out." Those words were followed by, "Do you need anything while I'm out?" I responded, "Nope. I just got everything I needed from you today and beyond." It gave me incredible strength to know that my wife believed in me to do what we had agreed would be my responsibility for the foreseeable future. Amen for Bonnie, once again.

I was very angry at losing my job, but I wasn't done with the big guy. Shortly after my last meeting with the big guy, I wrote him a letter reminding him that he had promised me some equity in a new bank division. I wanted my money, along with $250,000 severance pay. In exchange, I promised that I would not recruit, hire, or compete against him for a year. He took deep offense to the letter, viewed it as a threat, and had a law firm respond. In the end, I agreed to a one-year non-compete in exchange for a full year of compensation, benefits, and a few other things. Why would a hard guy like him give me that deal, especially when he had replaced the bank's CEO of fifteen years with one of his sons and given him nothing? It was because I had hired, trained, and earned the respect of every single salesperson in the bank. That and maybe a touch of guilt, but I can't speak for him on that. Remember the "win the crowd, win your freedom" lesson I learned when applying for Dean Junior College? Unfortunately for the bank, an angry, unemployed person in that position can cause serious problems.

It took me a long time to resolve my anger at the situation and people involved, but losing that job became a major turning point in my life, one that changed the way I earned a living forever. However, before I embarked on another direction, I decided to take some time off to think seriously about my life and my next career move.

Sealing My Criminal Record

As my job with the bank ended, I decided to tie up a loose end that had affected my self-esteem for a long time, that of my criminal record. It had continued to haunt me, even while I felt safely employed at the bank. This part of me was a fairly well-kept secret. I remember feeling the impact of this more than ten years after I was convicted. A prime example was when I volunteered to coach my son Chad's soccer team when Chad was five years old. I went to the first coaches meeting for a pep talk, collected my equipment, and received a packet of forms and information. The gentleman speaking said, "The first page in your packet is a BCI authorization form. You must sign and return this before entering the playing field." My heart dropped because a BCI form is for a criminal background check. I did not sign the form, but I did take the equipment and went home.

When Bonnie asked me how it went, I cried. I had done an incredible job of concealing my past for almost fifteen years and was not willing to jeopardize everything I had accomplished now. But what would I say to my five-year-old? I was consumed with guilt, regret, and fear because

I realized that my past would always be a part of my life. Again, I felt the old "cumulative effect of life's decisions." Bonnie, the practical one, came up with a solution, however. We listed her as the coach and sent in the form, then I went on to coach and had the time of my life. Once again, it was the people in my life who made the difference time and again—Amen for Bonnie.

That incident motivated me to have my criminal record sealed. The statute requires a waiting period of fifteen years, so my first petition to seal it was in 2001, fifteen years after my arrest in 1986. Unfortunately, I had failed to consider my five-year probationary period, which did not expire until April 1993, so I had to refile five years later in 2008. In 2008, my criminal record was officially sealed and behind me.

Coaching soccer with my son Chad

7

TIME OUT AND FIRST ATTEMPTS AT SELF-EMPLOYMENT

Regrouping and Reconnecting

By 2003, Bonnie and I had three beautiful children, Chad (eight), Abby (six), and Ben (three), and I had been married for over eleven years. Our family structure is paternalistic, something Bonnie wanted. Her priorities are God, husband, children, and then work. Bonnie came from a family structure similar to mine, and I am very close to her parents, Tom and Linda. Linda was a hairdresser who also sold Mary Kay, and Tom was a successful businessman who worked for one company his entire career. They have a very comfortable upper-middle-class life and have become good friends with my parents. Tom has always been great to me. They are both loving, kind, and very close to their daughters: Bonnie, Jill, and Tricia. Tom was distraught when I left the bank and decided to become an entrepreneur because he is a zero-risk kind of guy. I appreciated that. He wanted what he thought was best for our young family. But that was based on what he knew, not what I knew. My dad encouraged me to take a shot at it. Bonnie, as always, was 100% supportive and confident of my abilities to provide for the family.

When I lost my job, I realized I had been measuring my self-worth solely by material things and professional successes, not by my relationship with my family or contribution to society. I knew something had to change, and once I lost my job, I had time to think about my next move and reconnect with my family. A long family vacation sounded like the place to start, so I decided to rent a 32-foot RV and spend the next 35 days on a cross-country trip with my family.

The RV Trip

Bonnie, our family's organizer who also pays the bills and keeps our household going, immediately planned for the RV and the trip. She plotted a course that would take us from Rhode Island through Virginia, Tennessee, Mississippi, Louisiana, Texas, New Mexico, Arizona, Colorado, Utah, Wyoming, South Dakota, and Ohio.

While on the road, I made a pact with myself to do everything I could to avoid getting another job. I was determined to take a shot at living by my own hand as an entrepreneur or at least an equity holder going forward. I did not know what that would look like, but I had to try. One of my goals for the trip was to keep track of my feelings about going out on my own. I kept in touch with Tommy Couture, who was still working at the bank and wanted to join me in this next chapter of our lives. I also began a journal that described the sights and experiences of our trip and my thoughts about my family, career, personal goals, and philosophy. The journal extended to 2013, and some of the entries will be referred to in later chapters of this book.

Another equally important goal for the trip was to become closer to my family, especially Abby. Of my three children, she is the one most different from me, and I wanted to find more things in common with her. Also, we seemed to have more conflict than the boys and I, maybe because we're both strong-willed middle children. She was opinionated, determined, and driven. I had a different relationship with the boys: I could solve most problems with a look or a statement like, "We are definitely not doing that," and they would say, "Yes, sir." With Abby, it was more like a hostage negotiation. She will laugh when she reads this as she knows how much I love her; now we are very close.

Our trip began on June 6, 2003. As we drove south, we saw the Grand Old Opry of Nashville, the birthplace of Elvis in Tupelo; the French Quarter, alligators, and bayous of New Orleans; and the Alamo. Next, we attended the annual Texas Folklife Festival in San Antonio, the Carlsbad Caverns in New Mexico, and the Painted Desert. At the Petrified Forest in Arizona, we witnessed the plight of Navaho and Apache Indians there. Next were the Grand Canyon and Mesa Verde, where I had a great Father's Day gift: we spent the night at the Cortez Best Western and ate at a nice Italian restaurant! We loved the RV life but were ready for a break. As we continued to travel west, we enjoyed the red clay of Utah, the snow in Wyoming, the Badlands, and Mount Rushmore in South Dakota. Our last real tourist stop was at the Football Hall of Fame in Canton, Ohio, where we all dressed in Patriots Gear. Chad was a HUGE football fan, and the Pats had just won the Super Bowl. Our favorite QB Tom Brady was featured everywhere, and we walked around like we owned the place. Go Pats.

Throughout the trip, we were amazed at how friendly and thoughtful people acted in the South and Southwest and how clean the facilities were compared to our area of the country. We enjoyed meeting other RVers, and the kids began to get along better, making friends and becoming more outgoing. Chad and Ben became better swimmers, and Chad became quite an entrepreneur selling baseball flipbooks. Abby caught her first fish, which we ate for dinner. We took countless photos of all activities and went camping, fishing, touring, swimming, horseback riding, saw a rodeo, and climbed many hills. The children tried new foods and saw a large assortment of animals, including prairie dogs, black bears, rattlesnakes, bats, and—up-close—bison, mule deer, elk, and wolves.

Journal Musings

- I am reading about the Beatitudes, and they are resonating with me. Happiness comes from what you focus on, not how much you have.
- Life is beautiful and unpredictable. I am trying to go with the flow.
- The kids are great—I have never felt so close to them. Abby and I are sharing much more. I need to continue to cultivate our relationship.
- I find myself constantly reminding myself and the children why I wanted to take this trip. I tell them I love them incessantly. I want as many "moments" with them as possible. I apologize for all the time I spent working, and I promise them we will do this again.
- Horses—I would love to learn to ride and teach the kids a simpler way of life. Someday I will have a ranch with horses, even if it's a second home. I want to take more long trips as the kids get older. It will require a different way of making money and a more flexible career, but I know I can make it happen.
- It's time to put [the bank] where it belongs—in the past.

- The kids were bouncing off the walls from seeing all the animals [Wyoming]. This is what the trip was all about—new experiences, family bonding, and appreciating nature and our country.
- The scenery and desolate roads are an excellent opportunity to let your mind wander to new places— something that I will dearly miss.

An Incredible Experience in Albuquerque

Our family was enjoying a pancake breakfast one Wednesday morning in Albuquerque when a tall, powerfully built man came to our table. He complimented Bonnie and me on how well-behaved our children were and remarked how nice it was to see a family enjoying a meal, let alone traveling the country together. Then, he asked us if we had heard of Mr. Rogers, a Presbyterian minister who had a children's TV show. I told him I had grown up watching that TV show and was very familiar with some of its great lessons.

The man became excited and explained that he was also a pastor and fan of Mr. Rogers, then sat down and proceeded to share what he thought were important lessons to be learned and practiced. I should have been taken aback by his forwardness but felt very comfortable in his presence, and I remember the lessons he shared on how to treat children:

1. Talk to children every day about what's going on in their lives. But, more importantly, listen to what they have to say.
2. Tell them they do not have to be superstars in everything they do to earn your love and that you love and accept them as they are.
3. Tell them that you respect them as a person and that they have rights, too.
4. Let them know that you are their friend and want to help them in any way you can. Of course, that does not mean you abrogate your responsibility as a parent, but you can still be friends as well.
5. Tell them you and God love them and hug them every day.

I found myself being drawn to his presence and listened intently to every word. At that point, the kids and Bonnie left, and I continued to converse with this man alone. We discussed our views on geopolitics and agreed that people of faith could work together to define themselves by the peace they have created versus the wars they have won or lost. Finally, I told him how I had left my job of thirteen years, and he offered me this advice:

You are a strong and intelligent man, and you will be better off. Look at what you have already gained—perspective. Losing your job happened to you for a reason. You have a great attitude about letting go of the past. Right now, enjoy your family, and in time things will become clearer. God loves you. Take care of yourself and your family, and things will work out.

I almost cried when he said those words. I felt like a stranger had lifted an enormous burden. I wanted to hug him, something I would never do ordinarily, so I stood and offered my hand in thanks. Then an amazing thing happened; the pastor stood and embraced me and began to pray as he held me. He said, "Lord, thank you for this beautiful day. Please put your hand on this young man and his family. Amen." Then he added, "Drive slow; you are in no hurry. Be safe, and God bless you." For the next few days, I was on such an emotional high. God had sent this man, no doubt about it. Thank you, Lord.

First Attempts at Self-Employment

Flipping Houses

I was being paid under my non-compete agreement with the bank, so I felt like I could try my hand at something new—flipping houses. Real estate was booming, and I had the cash to get started, so I told Bonnie I would buy some distressed houses and fix them up for resale. She said, "I love you, but honey, you don't know how to fix anything!" I didn't own tools or even a lawnmower and was the least handy human on the planet. Bonnie took care of everything around the house and yard—all the basics. I drove my kids to school for four years and used the car's GPS to do it every day! Like I said, sales and teaching people how to sell was what I did best. That was pretty much the extent of my skills repertoire. If not for those skills, I would probably be homeless.

So, I went to a Donald Trump seminar in New York City with a realtor and heard several experts talk about flipping houses. After listening to them, the entrepreneur in me decided on a better way. I thought, "What if I had a listing of a house that needed a lot of work, but the seller was in a hurry?" With that in mind, I bought a house for $150,000 that was probably worth $225,000 to $230,000, but it was so dirty and cluttered that you couldn't even walk through it. I held $10,000 in escrow when I bought it and told the seller I would not release it until the house was thoroughly cleaned and decluttered. After the seller complied, I released the money and immediately re-listed the house. I was there painting the dining room when a young man who had just inherited some money came by and asked if it was for sale. I sold it that day, making around $40,000 in profit.

The next house I bought was not selling because the sewage system, which ran right by the house, was not connected to it, and because of that, the property was not eligible for most types of mortgage financing. A lack of mortgage financing dramatically limited the appeal of the listing. It was also the worst advertised house in the world. I walked up to the owner and said, "This is what I'm willing to do. I'll pay you cash," and I closed as soon as we received the title search. To sell the house, I changed the wording on the advertisement to "all financing available, zero down" and connected the house to the sewer. After spending $4,000, I had a buyer within a week.

I flipped a total of five houses, looking for situations that didn't require tools and taking out a $250,000 line of credit against my house. I became very confident, even approaching my dad and offering to pay him interest plus points if he financed a deal. My dad made about $25,000 on a couple of deals, and he was psyched. My older brother approached me for the same kind of deal and made several thousand dollars as a result. At one point, I had four houses going at once and owed $1.2 million, but my wife never said a word.

The Bank Deal

While I was flipping houses, the former CEO of the bank, not the big guy, called me and said, "we are going to buy a bank in Rhode Island, and we want you to run sales. You can bring Tommy with you." Tommy Couture was my wife's first cousin, a very smart and ambitious guy who caught the garter at my wedding and played football for Bryant. He went to work for the bank despite my warnings, and his career took off quickly. That dude was the real deal, a straight sales OG (original gansta). After I left, Tommy was promoted to the head of the commercial lending department there. But he was unhappy at the bank and wanted to come and flip houses with me, so Tommy quit his corporate gig and followed me into the real estate business.

The CEO offered to give me two and a half percent equity in the bank and 60% of my salary while he negotiated the purchase of the new bank. Once it closed, I had to make an additional five-year commitment to stay and help with the transition of the second sale as his group was thinking they could flip it after boosting revenue. He was willing to give us financial consideration in return for a commitment to the bank when he purchased it. The bank deal never closed, but Tommy and I received our agreed-upon payments for ten months, along with severance pay from the bank and money I earned flipping houses. The CEO had been a man of his word, another tough business guy but an honest guy. I learned an important lesson from him: your word means everything in business. We had a saying, "Let your yes be your yes, and your no be your no." In other words, the old, "If I tell you it's raining, you don't need to put your hand out the window."

TNT Mortgage Consulting and the Lawsuit

When my non-compete ended with the bank, I started TNT Mortgage Consulting with Tommy. We offered consulting and recruiting services for banks, mortgage companies, and credit unions. The name TNT came from Tim and Tom. We recruited away about fifteen out of the 42 loan officers still working at the bank, and rightfully, the big guy was pissed. My bad beast was working overtime, and I couldn't feed him fast enough. For a while, I just let him run wild. We earned $7,500 for loan officers and $12,000 for managers we recruited and trained—a total score for our newly formed business.

Our big break came from the owner of a large mortgage company, a multi-state operation based in Connecticut. The owner had received a mail piece I had created, and he called to see what we could do for him. Our company consisted only of me, Tom, and our marketing manager/ receptionist. Our office was tiny and located in a not-so-nice strip mall between a consignment store and a hair salon in Cranston, Rhode Island. The owner wanted to meet with us at our office, so I became concerned with appearances. After he arrived and asked several questions, he said, "You guys seem like you're pretty motivated, and I like what you're trying to do. If I give you $20,000, you'll train all my people, right?" I said, "Right, but I will need $5,000 today."

He wrote us the check, and we were off to the races! He hired us to do one-day workshops at a hotel or the mortgage company, and I did all the training. I felt great. Someone was willing to pay me for sales training.

I was just blown away. I had been an employee my whole life. Suddenly, I was an entrepreneur with multiple income sources—money from flipping houses, money from the pending bank deal with the CEO, and now from TNT Mortgage Consulting.

One major problem popped up. As I said, the big guy was pissed, and he decided to sue us for $250,000. He couldn't do anything about the recruiting, but he did have a legitimate gripe about me using the training manual I wrote while working at the bank. Stupidly, I used that manual verbatim in my contracts with the companies I recruited for, so he sued me for intellectual property theft. They had very expensive lawyers, but they weren't very sophisticated themselves, and—to make a long story short—they settled for a fraction of the suit. I viewed it as tuition. As I said, that was a stupid mistake. I could have easily tweaked it to avoid a problem, but I was caught up in feeding the bad beast, and I let that cloud my judgment—a mistake I would not make again. Nothing good happens in high-stakes business when you're operating from a place of anger. Angry people make dumb decisions. And I was case in point.

RV stop- The Badlands

Family photo- Outer Banks, NC

RV stop- Mt. Rushmore

RV stop- Utah

Driving in RV with my daughter Abby

RV stop- Grand Tetons

RV stop- Grand Canyon

PART THREE
CONTROLLING THE CHAOS

"Progress always involves risks. You can't steal second base and keep your foot on first."
—Frederick B. Wilcox

8

ASTONISH RESULTS

Adam

I was super impressed with Adam DeGraide long before he approached me to go into business with him. He was younger than me by a few years, but he was already wildly successful in his first two start-ups, BZ Results and Astonish Entertainment. He sold BZ Results in 2006 and had started Astonish Entertainment, a recording company, in 2005. We met through our wives and daughters when I was in the middle of my one-year non-compete. At that time, Adam was dialed in on his faith, a devout, conservative, active Christian, and we immediately became good friends.

Soon after we met, my wife convinced me we should spend New Year's Eve at the DeGraide's second home in Florida. That would be the first time our families spent any real time together. While in Florida, we went on VIP tours to all the theme parks and ate at expensive restaurants—luxury all the way. Every time I tried to pay my share, he would say, "Oh, don't worry, I got it," and those were not small bills. At the end of the week, feeling guilty, I asked one more time if I could pay for at least some of the things, but he refused, finally allowing me to make a small donation to his church instead. Two weeks later, he invited Bonnie and I to the Super Bowl in Jacksonville, Florida, where the Patriots were playing the Eagles. Once again, he insisted on paying for everything. As it turned out, his company had invited 100 of their customers to the Super Bowl, giving them (and us) all-expense-paid packages, including suites on the cruise ships and after-game party tickets. Adam's generosity amazed me, but the more I got to know him, the more I realized no one paid when they traveled with Adam.

Adam and I became close, and after a year or so, he told me he was getting ready to sell his first company, BZ Results. Selling that company would be the first of three strategic exits for him. BZ Results was a digital marketing company assisting car dealers; Adam started BZ after a successful stint selling radio ads. Both his dad and grandfather were well-known radio DJs. Adam's plan was to immediately begin a second digital marketing and software company after the sale of BZ while simultaneously growing the music label. Since I already had my mortgage business up and running, we could introduce these services to our existing customers. We would take what I had developed with TNT, incorporate it into our digital marketing strategy, and I would run sales and marketing. I liked the idea but was still committed to the bank deal with the CEO, which included a five-year commitment after the bank was purchased. In the end, the bank deal fell through. I called Adam, whose offer was still open, and the rest is history.

Adam and I started two companies together, Astonish Results in 2005 and Crystal Clear Digital Marketing in 2013. Both provided digital marketing, software, and consulting services. Astonish served the local insurance agent community, and Crystal Clear worked with elective medical practices. Both Astonish and Crystal Clear made it into the prestigious Inc 500 and were sold to different private equity firms. The second company was purchased by a firm started by Jerry Jones, owner of the Dallas Cowboys. Together Adam and I fought many battles, risked everything more than once, and formed a bond few people share. He mentored me in entrepreneurship 101, then 201, then 301, and 401, and his mentorship changed my life in many ways.

Early Trials and Tribulations

The Astonish Results ownership consisted of five partners with varying degrees of equity. Adam and his former partner at BZ were the primary stakeholders. I was happy with that because this was my first rodeo as a shareholder, and Adam had been through this before. I believed in his vision, experience, and marketing savvy. Our first major challenge came when the real estate and mortgage market started to crash in 2006, leading to the massive financial crisis of 2008. That was a serious problem. We had all these big contracts in place, and the companies started failing at an alarming rate. We needed to make a bold move. I was introduced to a local insurance agent in Massachusetts just as the state was preparing to deregulate the insurance market, which would attract companies like Geico. There would be a big marketing blitz as a result, making existing agents anxious and presenting an opportunity for Astonish. After meeting with the agent, I was convinced this was the direction we needed to take. Everyone agreed, and that move turned out to be the right one. Adam spent more and more time traveling with the music label, and we were forced to figure some things out without him. I was getting frustrated, mostly due to a lack of confidence, which created some pressure on the partnership. That situation would be the first of many dustups with Adam over the years.

When two people agree on everything, one of them is unnecessary. Fortunately, he and I were always able to work through the issues. That was not the same for all partners. We had one overbearing partner who was not operationally involved in the business. He had funded several companies after BZ, and I think the financial pressure from that caused him to behave erratically. We were not able to work through it, and as a result, we discontinued all compensation and functionally removed him from the business. That was tough stuff. Personally, I would never attempt to start a business like this without a partner. That said, you must choose your partners carefully. Once you share equity, that's it. You are married. The good news is we paid back his entire investment with interest, and he shared in the profits when we sold the business.

Feeling increasingly uncertain, I grew upset with Adam, who flew into Rhode Island to meet with the other partners and me. I confronted him, things escalated, and at one point, Adam stormed out of the meeting with John, the COO, running after him. Adam and I were both furious with one another. On a personal level, I was not doing a great job handling the pressure—drinking too much, poor diet. Excerpts from the following entry I made in my journal in October 2006 shows my state of mind:

God is great. Every day he reveals truths to me. He has done miracles in my life, [but] I struggle with every form of sin every day. My compulsion towards alcohol and an unhealthy diet keeps me from drawing closer to him. Some days I feel like a war is going on in my mind.

At the end of 2007, Adam, who had the most equity in the business, returned as CEO. This was a blessing on multiple fronts. One, we needed his full-time attention in our rapidly growing business. Two, Adam recognized my contribution to the company, and while the equity structure remained in place, he agreed to increase my compensation to match his own going forward. That worked for me.

As we worked together and got to know each other, Adam's trust in me grew. I worked hard to increase my value to the business. He helped me become an incredible speaker by his example and confidence in my abilities. That meant a lot. I'll never forget the first day that we were doing a big keynote speech in California in front of a bunch of insurance agents. We handled our speaking engagements for a long time by splitting the time. Typically, he would go first, then I would close it out. Prior to the event in California, we were having breakfast, and I was telling him what I thought I would say. He looked at me over his toast and said, "I don't care what you do. I'm going to leave after twenty minutes and go to Las Vegas. You don't mind if I blast when I'm done, do you?" I said, "I guess that's fine," but I went into panic mode, thinking, "Oh boy, now these people will find out I don't know anything!" Then I realized that Adam was letting me know he trusted me to carry on alone, and I gave the best speech in my life. When the MC who introduced us went to the podium after our talk, he said, "I don't know about you guys, but after listening to Tim, I think I need a cigarette!"

An Unfair Advantage

In its July 2009 issue, *Rough Notes* magazine featured an article written by Nancy Doucette, "Unfair Advantage," on

Astonish Results. Interviews with Adam, myself, and our customers talked about how the playing field had changed because modern consumers were now using the internet as a primary means of searching for insurance. Astonish used software to manage all sales and marketing activities, and interviews with customers shared how their business had increased after working with Astonish Results. One company claimed a 300% increase in the amount of new business. *Rough Notes* magazine is the top publication in the insurance industry, and we received a lot of publicity from the story.

Articles about Astonish were written in several other magazines as well, talking about how we were disrupting the way marketing had been done in the insurance business. For example, the cover story for November 1, 2009, *Insurance Journal* was an article about Astonish, "The Face of Freakin' Agency Marketing." Another magazine, the *National Underwriter/American Agent and Broker,* wrote an article in August 2010, "Astonish Shakes Up Agency Marketing with Aggressive, Web-Centric Approach."

Astonish Results was making a big splash. Apart from the services we provided, it was the most incredible sales and marketing engine I had ever seen.

Adam and I were the faces of the business, giving presentations and interviews, but while my confidence grew, I sometimes felt like an imposter. I had this crazy past, and yet I was advising insurance agency owners on how to run their business. The problem was we were right. The world had changed for these folks. I spent more and more time traveling, missing my family, and at times neglecting them; my mind was on Astonish 24/7, even at home. I struggled; it was like being on a treadmill with no off button. The business was booming, but Bonnie and I had real problems. In 2009, Chad was thirteen, Abby was twelve, and Ben was eight, and I had to remind myself often of my priorities: God, Bonnie, family, and then work.

A Culture of Results at All Costs

Astonish was growing but not without challenges. In his previous business, Adam and his partners had successfully utilized a relatively new way of thinking about financing growth. The idea of leasing or factoring had historically been reserved for large capital purchases like commercial refrigeration, copy machines, and physical items. So, if a business wanted to finance the purchase, they would get the money from a leasing company, pay the vendor, and then make installment payments to the leasing company. As far as I know, Adam and his partners were the first to apply this mechanism to a software and marketing contract. In theory, and for us in practicality, this was an effective way to get cash into the business quickly. The customer would sign a multi-year contract, we got our money upfront, and payments were made to the leasing company. The downside was a more complex sales process, more pressure on the customer or vendor relationship to make timely payments, and increased risk of legal issues. We understood that and decided it was worth it. The trickier part was responsibly managing the influx of cash. We had some growing to do on this front. Hence the New England Patriots and Orlando Magic luxury boxes, extravagant customer events, and a culture of work hard/play harder.

Follow-Up is Punishment for Not Closing on Day One

At Astonish, we had an aggressive sales culture, mainly because that was who we were at the core, aggressive sales dudes. We spent a ton of time developing our sales processes. Everything was scripted, all presentations were uniformly delivered, every possible question and objection thought out, and responses rehearsed. We left nothing to chance. It started at the top. For example, I was on a second in-person visit to a large insurance agency. I got close the first time but walked away empty-handed. This time I went with the attitude that "I'm not leaving here again without a contract." After 90 minutes or so, I was told, "We're going to do it. Just give us some more time." I said, "I can't do it.

I'm not leaving," and I walked up to him, knelt before him in front of his entire executive team, and said, "I'm begging you for your own good. Don't ask me to leave again." He tried to make me get up, but I refused, and he finally signed the contract. I truly believed it was in his best interest, and I would have let us both down if I had walked away. And I was all done "following up." I recognize to many people this sounds crazy. "Why would I humiliate myself like that?" The answer is simple—either he was going to sell me on *no*, or I was going to sell him on *yes*. The rest was irrelevant; just get it done.

We were the leading company in digital services for insurance agents, and our confidence led to tough contracts. Imagine that you were going to sign a three or five-year contract for digital marketing services and CRM software, and by the way, you must personally guarantee the contract. We would also need your social security number and tax returns. If you failed to pay us, we could sue you personally.

If anyone defaulted on their contract, we would threaten suit as soon as they became 60 days delinquent. Then, they would have to decide whether to hire a lawyer and defend the suit or honor the contract and comply with the terms of the agreement. In addition, all the contracts stated they had to be litigated in Rhode Island, which made it even more difficult for clients to defend the lawsuit or countersuit. Of course, these contracts were developed over ten years, and we considered every possible way someone could exploit them. Every business contract I have ever read is written in the business's best interest, not that of the customers.

Enter an attorney from Dallas, Texas, who represented three or four clients (out of 700 plus) looking to get out of their contracts. Full disclosure: Adam, correctly, was against the settlements. His philosophy was "give a mouse a cookie, and he'll want a glass of milk." This freaking ambulance chaser from Texas started running pay-per-click ads on Google, saying, "Want to get out of your Astonish contract? I've successfully settled. Call me."

The most uncomfortable day at Astonish came when this idiot represented nine of our clients, and we had to go into forced mediation. He had made a demand on our business and said, "I represent all these people, and this is how much money I want for each one of them." We said, "We're not doing that. We'll go to court." Typically, you must go through forced mediation with a judge mediator as part of that process. The Dallas lawyer showed up with the group he represented, and I had to sit in a room in front of nine people who wanted to kill me. Dallas made his opening statements, and you would have thought I was the devil himself by the time he was done.

I represented Astonish in all things legal. I had been through a lot in my life, and while this was an intimidating process, I had seen worse. The judge said, "OK, Tim, are there any settlement offers that you want to make right now?" I said, "Yes, I'm grateful for your time today and for everyone who flew from all over the country, and I want to be clear that I am perfectly willing to accept everyone in this room back as a customer with no hard feelings whatsoever. All we ask is that each of them brings their accounts current."

Apparently, that was not the answer they were looking for, thus the beginning of a very long day.

Then everyone peeled off, and the judge spoke with them for fifteen minutes to see what they could move on. When she came back, the judge said, "There's a lot of emotion in that room right now. Is there anything you are willing to do?" At the end of that battle, we settled with one of the clients I thought had some legitimate concerns. But ALL other cases were dismissed through a summary judgment, and the clients eventually turned on the lawyer as he could not fulfill his promise to win settlements for them.

Personnel Running Wild

The key players and performers at Astonish did not have clear boundaries for professionalism, which was on us. Part of the reason was bringing close friends or family into the business who were immature or otherwise ill-suited for the job. Another issue was that both Adam and I were somewhat freewheeling, spending money on luxuries and perks, enjoying the lifestyle afforded to us by the business to the max. Because of my background dealing with insanity, I became the "fixer" or "go-to" guy to deal with the problems that arose due to the culture we fostered.

We gave people a lot of leeway to ensure results, and occasionally, that would blow up in our faces. We had one guy who, at the age of twenty-one, was a highly gifted, confident sales dude. We put him on the road five days a week, paid him over $250,000 a year, and prayed he was mature enough to keep it together personally. Talent-wise, we had zero doubt in his ability. One day, he called me with a problem. He said, "Tim, you know that deal I signed on Friday? We have a problem." Picture a local insurance agency in the middle of nowhere. He presented a few days before and signed the agent, whose daughter worked in the agency. He took the daughter out that night, and she left her car at the insurance agency. They spent the night partying together, and then he dropped her off at the agency the next morning. The following day, he flew to New Orleans for Mardi Gras. Unfortunately for us, his car was vandalized while he was gone. Someone had stolen the insurance agent's tax returns, social security number, and contract with Astonish. I had the hard job of apologizing to the agency owner, but thankfully he was OK with it, and we were able to move on. I wanted to fire this guy more than once, but Adam was the ultimate believer in redemption. Me, not so much.

The Story of the Scorpion and the Frog

A scorpion wants to cross a river but cannot swim, so it asks a frog to carry it across. The frog hesitates, afraid that the scorpion might sting it, but the scorpion promises not to, pointing out that it would drown if it killed the frog in the middle of the river. The frog considers this argument sensible and agrees to transport the scorpion. Midway across the river, the scorpion stings the frog anyway, dooming them both. The dying frog asks the scorpion why it stung despite knowing the consequence, to which the scorpion replies: "I am sorry, but I couldn't resist the urge. It's in my nature."

The sales guy was a scorpion, so what did we expect? Finally, after eight years and many conditions he rarely met, we fired him. And as outrageous as it might seem, our attitude was as always, "Well, nobody got killed."

Our top guy was the most tenacious, intense sales guy I have ever met. Tommy called me one night/morning at around 3 a.m. You would think that was highly unusual. I answered, and he said, "I have good news and bad news," and described the events of that evening. We had just hired a new sales guy, and Tommy took him to shadow a closing meeting in Atlanta. Tom closed the deal, and afterward, they went out to celebrate with one of our existing local clients. Unfortunately, they ended up at an after-hours bar notorious for a high volume of police stops. As soon as they pulled out of the parking lot, they were pulled over, and our newly minted trainee was arrested, charged with drunk driving, and put in lockup. As a result, he lost his license and job with Astonish because he could no longer travel and rent cars. I asked Tommy, "How is this good news?" He replied, "Well, nobody got killed," to which I responded, "Great job on that deal, keep me posted." And I went back to bed.

Landing the Plane

In 2011, Adam and I agreed it was time to sell Astonish, and we hired an investment banking firm to represent us in the sale. The business was doing well, but the cash demands to keep it going were becoming increasingly difficult. In addition, our personal and professional lives were chaotic and, at times, bordering on out of control. At the end of what folks refer to as the dog and pony show, where you crisscross the country trying to convince investors to buy/ invest in the business, we had two private equity firms very interested. We settled on a number with the top bidder and began the due diligence process to close. Not an easy thing to do. Even the best-laid plans can blow up when you are a former convicted felon. Because we were not selling the whole business and would remain as officers in the new company, we went through a ton of scrutiny, including a questionnaire related to our pasts. When I saw the question, "Have you ever been convicted of a felony?" my heart sank because we were talking about losing millions of dollars if my record became an issue. After much consternation, I told Adam I would not lie and would accept the outcome, even if it included recusing myself from the deal. It is during times like these where you discover your real friends. As I was crying on the phone, Adam calmly said, "I won't let you do that. If they don't want to make a deal with you in it, f--- them. I'm not doing it." Through much negotiation, bluffing, and posturing, Adam consummated the sale, including me as an officer in the company.

Adam and I remained with Astonish as employees and board members for a while but eventually left, as these two groups of humans—the guys who start companies and the guys who buy them—aren't always meant to co-exist in the wild. And that entire experience was wild.

Mic'd up in Providence for first lecture as Astonish president. Bonnie brought Ben by for moral support.

Giving back with Adam DeGraide and the crew at Astonish

Me and Chad in the Patriots luxury box

Me and my man Adam DeGraide

All dressed up with Adam DeGraide

Shaking up an industry with Adam and
John Boudreau

TECHNOLOGY

GETTING RESULTS

Astonish exec shares lessons learned from working with hundreds of agency customers

Media day with John Boudreau, COO Astonish Results

9

REVISITING PRIORITIES

Keeping my priorities straight has always been an ongoing struggle for me, an ongoing battle between the two beasts. However, as I grow older, I better understand who I am and have a greater appreciation for the importance of my wife, family, friends, and faith. The whole thing is a constant battle, going up and down the spectrum of normalcy and insanity.

My Marriage

On June 9, 2013, I made one last entry in the journal I began in 2003:

I just returned from a family vacation in Aruba with the whole family, including Bonnie's parents, sisters, and kids.

Disaster!

Marriage—Falling apart—on the brink of a divorce.

Faith—Virtually non-existent.

Health—overweight, sick all the time. BAD!!

That was not the first time my life had been in turmoil. When I was on the road with Astonish Results, my absence and preoccupation with the job created serious problems within my marriage. Before Astonish, I had never been on a business trip in my life, but within two months, I was flying three to four times a week and was sometimes gone for the entire week. I was terrible; sometimes, I did not even bother to tell Bonnie where I was going. I was awful about communicating with her while on the road and only sent her random text messages. Bonnie was used to having me home all the time, so it was a huge change for her and the children.

When I did return home, usually on a Friday afternoon or Saturday morning on a red-eye flight, I would face all sorts of household issues. Bonnie and I would argue, go to our corners, and I would leave again. I was not just gone physically; I was gone mentally, both at home and while traveling. I had never owned a business before and had allowed it to become my life; it was all I wanted to talk about. The children saw and heard our fights, and we had to own our behavior, telling them that we knew it was wrong.

When Astonish was sold in 2011, our relationship became even worse as I had no plan or direction and was just hanging around the house thinking, drinking, and creating tension. Finally, I had what some people call a nervous breakdown and checked myself into a hospital. I received outpatient treatment consisting of individual and group counseling, staying there during the day and returning home at night for around ten days. Our marriage had become so fragile that Bonnie and I talked about whether I should come home at all. My wife and I have a bond, two souls that will be connected forever. Our relationship is intense, which can be very good or bad, with two strong-willed, independent personalities.

After my breakdown, we agreed to go to counseling, and the counselor talked about the contract that Bonnie and I had made years before. He said, "You had a contract that is now twenty to 25 years old, and it sounds to me like each of you wants to renegotiate that agreement." We knew what we had to do when he framed it that way, although it was tough. We renegotiated our contract because certain things that were OK then were not OK now.

By 2013, my life was at another low; thus, the journal entry. I was in my mid-40s, at home with a wife and three teenagers, and had some cash from the sale of Astonish. But I was still searching. What brought me out of my low was starting another company, creating a new purpose— Crystal Clear—and returning to work. Once that happened, I realized I was simply not wired to function without a challenge; I had to work to keep sane. Crystal Clear was a different kind of company, though, and at that time, my relationship with Bonnie began to improve.

Before leaving the subject of my marriage, I want to mention my commitment to Bonnie and hers to me through all the difficult times. Our fidelity to one another was a rope that kept us together. During my time at Astonish and since then, I have traveled hundreds of times; never once was I tempted to be unfaithful to my wife. I learned that from my dad, who expressed his opinion on the subject when I was young, and the Bill Clinton/Monica Lewinsky affair had come out. My dad said to me, "I really don't understand, Tim, how someone who could have so much—as president of the United States—would be willing to throw that away for three minutes of pleasure." That statement stuck with me my whole life. I was never going to throw away years of history for a few moments of pleasure.

Faith

My wife's priorities have always been God, husband, family, and work, in that order. I agree that God, Bonnie, family, and then work should be my priorities, but unlike Bonnie, I have rarely managed to keep them in order. I have never met anyone with more blind faith and positivity about the big things in life. Being married to someone like me is not easy. It takes an extraordinary person to handle my level of intensity, something I believe Bonnie is both attracted to and dismayed by depending on the situation. There is a side of Bonnie that was attracted to "bad boys" when she was younger. I had the propensity to be a dangerous human;

someone who would act boldly and get caught with a bunch of money and drugs could also be someone who started a company if he got his life organized. Bonnie liked that kind of adrenaline in her life, could handle it, and is grateful for the rewards associated with that. We now live in our dream home on the water with no mortgage. But I am sure that her faith has a lot to do with her ability to stand by me despite our ups and downs. A journal entry I made several years ago still stands true today:

Bonnie is so loving and forgiving. She is a great mother, best friend, passionate partner, and true community leader. Her selfless approach to life perfectly reflects her obedience and commitment to her faith.

Bonnie was raised in the Catholic church and always attended, but my beliefs and attendance have always been inconsistent. I do believe in God because I refuse to accept that humans are the result of two rocks being smashed against each other. But God and religion have often taken a back seat in my life because my mind is wired to work; I need to work and am constantly working on something.

The more I became involved in church as an adult, the more I started to judge Christianity by the people who espouse the faith, and I have struggled mightily for the last five to seven years trying to disassociate the two. People are fallible. That's why we need to have faith. I have faith but struggle with it daily, but I believe there is more to life than what's on earth.

My mom was always involved in the church, regardless of what was going on in her personal life; my dad came along later. Sometimes, they can come across as overly judgmental Christians to me, and I have respectfully challenged them on that. When I see Christians making choices entirely at odds with their faith when no one is looking and then judging people who do the same, I get turned off. I believe in taking personal responsibility for your actions and worrying about yourself. However, I also realize that none of us are perfect, and my parents have seen their share of challenges in life. That said, everything I am I owe to my parents. While I struggle with my spirituality, which my parents would put as a top priority, marriage and family are values that run deep in Bonnie and me, thanks to parents on both sides.

Parenting to Break the Cycle

Our first child, Chad, was born by then (1995), Abby (born in 1997) was on the way, and Ben would make his appearance in 2000.

When my children were twelve years old, I showed them my criminal record and said, "This is inside you." I talked about inherited traits from parents and grandparents and explained the challenges that my mother went through. Then I described what I went through and said:

This is what your father is capable of, so by virtue of that, you may have inherited some of my traits. You can go through life the hard way or the really hard way. The hard way is doing the right thing, being a good person, and understanding that if you give in to your worst impulses, they could get you in a lot of trouble. The really hard way is to give in to those impulses, make really bad choices, and do the wrong thing because that is what I did, and my criminal record is proof of what I am capable of doing. And there are lifetime consequences as a result.

"Do you understand?" I asked my children after the disclosure. Each child had a slightly different reaction, but they were all very quiet at first and then said they understood and would never do anything like that. So, while I think it was a lot for them to process, I also think it was entirely appropriate, and I would not change my decision to have that talk with them.

Knock on wood, a lot of time has passed, and through the entire time the children lived with us, we never had one drug or alcohol incident. Chad is now 26, Abby is 24, and Ben is 21 and in college, but when they were growing up, our children and their friends knew where we stood and what the boundaries were. We had a pool in the backyard where the kids hung out with their friends in the summer, and I got to know all of them well. Some of the high school kids would come over with a duffel bag, and I would say, "Are you studying tonight?" They would say, "What do you mean, Mr. Sawyer?" and I would reply, "You probably don't need that. Why don't you put it outside?" They were respectful of that because they knew where I stood.

Because of my experiences and Bonnie's maternal gifts, we were very in tune with our kids. We gave them plenty of room to develop their own identity. It wasn't always perfect, but I am proud of who my children have become. I have screwed up as a parent many times, but I'm OK with that because I own it and consider it a learning experience. I say, "I'm sorry. I blew that bad. I wish I could get it back, but I can't."

10

CRYSTAL CLEAR—A DIFFERENT KIND OF COMPANY

I n October 2013, Adam and I founded and incorporated our second company together, Crystal Clear Digital Marketing, headquartered in Orlando, Florida. As with Astonish Results, Adam was CEO/Founder, and I was President/Co-Founder. Once again, Tommy Couture was involved along with Joe Amaral from Astonish. Joe was a strong ops guy and a big part of our success in these ventures.

Crystal Clear provided digital marketing services and technology to elective medical practices across the US and Canada. We used the basic principles developed at B.Z. and Astonish based on the following philosophy. Every business must do three things well: find, sell, and keep more customers profitably. More importantly, we applied lessons learned from our mistakes at Astonish; we revised our business format with less aggressive sales and contracts and developed a more customer-centric model.

Crystal Clear Versus Astonish Results

When we started Crystal Clear, we toned down the out-of-control behavior and spending prevalent at Astonish. Spending was more controlled—no more luxury boxes at ball games, discretionary credit cards, or carrying customers' financial information around in a bag. Our success at Astonish was driven by making and spending money; it was all about seeing how far we could take it. Of course, we wanted to be financially successful at Crystal Clear, but we knew it was time to grow up a bit and become more responsible.

In addition to becoming more financially accountable, we also changed how we dealt with our customers. At Astonish, we had a lot of litigation because of our onerous contracts, and we quickly threatened our customers if they defaulted. However, suing customers is a tricky business that did not always end well, so we became more consumer-friendly with Crystal Clear customers. In the seven-plus years that we ran Crystal Clear, we avoided litigation at all costs, at times to our detriment. People can be crazy, but our position was: suing customers can be bad for business. So, once again, it was time to make the donuts.

Personally, I knew I couldn't go through another seven years like we did at Astonish. My mental and physical health had suffered, as well as my marriage. During the Crystal Clear project, Adam married Krystle, a beautiful woman with exceptional business savvy. He now had young children at home, and his focus and demeanor reflected that.

In our first company, Astonish, Adam and I had always done presentations together and were seen as the "face" of the business. At Crystal Clear, I assumed responsibility for that role exclusively. We discovered early on that presenting at medical conferences was the most effective way to get practices to sign in volume, so public speaking was vital for success. Before long, we were doing more than 50 conferences a year. We peaked at 70 plus conferences in 2019, the last year before COVID.

Approach to Public Speaking

In addition to providing actionable education to the folks who attended my talks, the secondary goal was to motivate them to visit us at our booth. It was a simple math equation. If there is a business interest attached to your speech, in general, one-third of the audience will not be interested, one-third will be inclined to listen, and the one-third in the middle need to be swayed. But it's the one-third inclined to respond who should get the most attention. When I discuss my approach to public speaking, I explain it this way: "What do I want people to think, what do I want them to feel, and what do I want them to do?" Everything I say in my presentations focuses on those three words: think, feel, and do. The only way to do that is to provide relevant data that is relatable to the majority of your audience, such as, "OK, guys, what I'm going to share with you today is what the fastest growing insurance agencies and medical practices consider to be the best practices in the country." Often after a presentation, sophisticated men and women would come up to me and say, "I don't exactly know what you do, but what you just said made sense. How do we get started?" Why? Because they had an emotional reaction and a connection with me as a human. And when you think in those terms, public speaking becomes very different. Now I'm not worried about everyone leaving a good survey. I'm there to get something done.

To this day, I've never written a speech. I rely heavily on well-crafted PowerPoints for talking points, but I struggle with lengthy notes or specific language. My unquiet mind is not suited for that. I think about my speech and then do it. It is not unusual for Bonnie to observe me staring out a window with a blank look on my face and then ask, "What are you doing?" I would reply, "I'm writing a speech." For her, hearing that was completely normal. She would even go so far as to say, "Let me know when you're done." If I sat down and tried to write an opening to a speech, I would struggle and get frustrated. For me, opening a talk depends on several factors, like the feeling I get looking around the room, the size of the crowd, and if people are on their iPads and not paying attention. I must get their attention—shock them. In most of the talks that I give, I don't even say the name of my company. I speak about principles. I need to create a scenario where folks believe I am sharing the ultimate truth. In other words, "This is how the world works … "

The largest audience I ever spoke to was in Washington, DC. The stage was huge, with over three thousand attendees, and the lights were so bright I couldn't see the crowd. Giant cranes with cameras on them would go up and down the aisles to get pictures of the attendee's reactions, but I felt like I needed to be closer to them to connect. So, I immediately walked off the stage and went down into the audience to give my speech. Then, when I was about to finish, I went back up on stage, got down on one knee, and said, "Listen, I'm literally begging you: do *not* disregard what we discussed today." Adam has often compared my speaking style to that of a gospel preacher. Many times, I have said to business audiences, "Can I get an amen?" Even the least religious folks in the audience would respond positively. That's when I knew I was in the zone.

A Great Company

Crystal Clear started signing customers in January of 2014. We were super aggressive on stage and in the booth and had a solid business model that required lots of podium time. As I mentioned, we did over 70 shows in 2019 with a team of six, including my son Chad, who has become an absolute rock star in his own right. To this day, he leads the sales team in revenue and contributes to the development of new team members. In the end, Crystal Clear was named Best Practice Marketing Company 2017 by *the* Aesthetic Industry Awards and the Top Aesthetic Service Provider 2016–2020 by Aesthetic Everything, the largest network of aesthetic professionals in the world. In addition, I was named Top President of 2017–2020 by Aesthetic Everything and had faculty credentials at 35 conferences and associations across the US. Two words that best describe Crystal Clear are: *well played*.

COVID and the Home Stretch

The world changed in March 2020 with the rise of COVID. Within two weeks, we were confronted with two significant challenges:

1. Almost 100% of our subscription-based customers were considered non-essential as they were all in elective medicine. As a result, they were all forced to close.
2. Seventy percent of our new client acquisitions came from trade shows, all canceled for the foreseeable

future. Out of necessity, I needed some help from the good beast.

Here is what we did.

Prologue | Strategy Adjustment Update | March 15, 2020— Present (COVID Era)

The strategy is predicated on one simple assumption: all early-stage marketing efforts would have to be internet-based for the foreseeable future. Our competitors would face the same challenge, and we needed to turn this to our advantage. Over the past seven years, we have built strong alliances with some of the top vendors in elective medicine. We provided zero-cost content and world-class speakers in exchange for database access. During COVID, we will:

1. Leverage our well-maintained database of prospects, including mobile numbers and email addresses gathered from the hundreds of trade shows. The mobile numbers are a game-changer during COVID.
2. Create and market effective educational programs as we have run many of them for the largest associations in the world. We know how to win the crowd.
3. Leverage strong brand recognition from the one million dollars a year investment in sales and marketing efforts.

4. Ask our friends for help. Some of the top doctors and surgeons in the US are strong non-paid vocal advocates. The trust in CCDM means more to them than a few shiny nickels. We will ask them for help, and they will be happy to do it.

5. Leverage the podcast. Created in early 2019, we have done more than 66 episodes interviewing some of the industry's biggest names and celebrity surgeons. Currently, the podcast has more than 28,000 unique downloads. But, most importantly, the motivation comes with the knowledge that we have a major challenge/opportunity on our hands, and it's not going away any time soon.

When looking at the list above, it's easy to say, "OK, that seems simple enough." Tactically speaking, it is straightforward. Practically speaking, our commitment to strong sales processes makes it all possible. If you have ever worked the booth at a trade show, you know how hard it can be—often boring when you go a day or two without talking to a single prospect, which happens more often than you think. The hardest part is staying focused, so you are physically and mentally at your best when getting a shot.

That said, when you walk the floor of a slow trade show, what do you see? You see empty booths (salespeople aren't all created equal), blurry eyes from a rough night, talking on phones, people playing with their iPads as the infrequent prospect strolls by, which is money lost. We treated trade shows very differently. We have three main objectives at trade shows:

1. Close somebody *at the show*. Conversations are great, but we need to find a way to pay for the $10,000 it costs to get there. We will be the first to show up and the last ones to leave, and *every* interaction matters. Making sales is serious business, and our sales guys know it. We have a saying, "Follow-up is punishment for not closing at the show."

2. Get their contact information—not just a random email for the practice or the business phone number. Get *their* personal contact information, cell phone, and email address.

3. Make a friend. Visit with your neighbor and get to know their business. You never know. But I know this: They sell to doctors and surgeons just like we do, which means they also have a database of a whole bunch of folks we would love to get in front of. That's worth talking about.

Before we move on from our three trade show objectives, I think it's worth taking a minute to talk about collecting personal contact information from skeptical prospects. First, we must recognize that this is a critical sales function. It is considered a very aggressive ask for doctors and surgeons, so we must do it with some finesse. People are funny about giving you their information. Some give it up quickly, while others act like you will use the information to rob their house.

If you have ever been in a position where you are required to obtain prospects' email addresses, you know how difficult this can be. First, you must get them to stop and talk to you—not an easy task. Then you must quickly build value in what you have to offer (your elevator pitch). Finally, you must build trust that you will not abuse their personal information. That is a tall order for many, impossible for most. Unfortunately, there is not enough emphasis in sales training programs on thinking about *exactly* what we will say when it counts. We call it situational football, and it requires practice. While getting a mobile number is a big ask, the more you make of it, the less likely you will get it. Think, "Would you mind passing me the ketchup? Here's why … "

My favorite personal move: take out your phone, pull up your contacts list, and say the following: "Hey, can I get your number so I can just text you to schedule a follow-up? I know you don't want me harassing everyone at the office. So, I'll text you mine right now in case you think of any questions." Hint: keep the tone of your voice calm and matter of fact. Try it. What do you have to lose? The freaking mobile number, that's what!

Armed with personal email addresses and mobile numbers, you can really cut down the time and money it costs chasing prospects after the fact—*a lot of time*! Said another way, a little extra sales work upfront makes a big difference in the long run. In the era of COVID, communication is king, and the ability to mass text is priceless!

Enter the ZOOM BOOM—and Stop Looking at Your Face

It is astounding how fast the entire world went virtual. Smart companies used the opportunity to change how they did business and saved a ton of money doing it.

Round one of the Zoom Boom was a little awkward. It was downright uncomfortable for those who had little to no experience with virtual meetings. Why? Because people can't stop staring at themselves. Selfies are one thing but staring at yourself for 90 minutes? As Joe Biden likes to say, "C'mon, man." But Zoom was new to most users, and like anything new, it took some getting used to. The challenge was to recreate the same excitement and enthusiasm that often follows a great in-person conference experience. Step one was to define what makes for a great conference experience.

Our strategy focused on three specific areas:

1. The content: We knew it had to be timely, relevant, and continuously updated to reflect the real-life conditions unfolding in different parts of the country. So, we tied most discussions to the re-opening phases defined by the CDC and the administration. Just repeating the same old topics from the shows was not going to work because there was way too much noise in the world. The content had to be compelling, and it had to be sold!

2. The speakers: We put a great deal of thought into who we wanted to have in our educational programs. While

the practice of using KOLs (key opinion leaders) is widely accepted, during COVID, it felt a little off the mark. We were convinced practice owners would be more drawn to down-to-earth providers experiencing success in the early stages of re-opening. That group was eager to prove their worth in our conversations, and they were willing to give their time and talent freely. When trying to reduce acquisition costs to zero (short-term), you must get creative. The process was like a VP pick. How can this person bring more people into our ecosystem? That was all that mattered.

3. The audience: Major consideration was given to expanding our reach and building our database. We understood that continuing to market solely to our existing database would be an exercise in diminishing returns. With no new shows on the horizon, expanding our reach would require a new approach. As I mentioned before, we had fortunately made many friends while flying around the country in our little traveling caravan; now, it was time to circle the wagons. You didn't have to be a rocket scientist to realize our vendor friends were dealing with the same issues whether they knew it or not. In hindsight, I'm not sure what some of them were thinking. Most resorted to furloughs, layoffs, and a hunker-down mentality; their fear of the unknown was causing a significant amount of panic in the vendor community.

In the two years leading up to the COVID pandemic, ROI (return on investment) from event marketing was slowly declining. The decline was the result of the proliferation of new shows (too many choices), an explosion in competition to the gold rush in elective medicine (too many vendors), and decreasing attendance. Many of my entrepreneur friends in our world were already in the process of cutting back on the number of shows while discussing ways to deal with the shifting dynamic. The problem was shows were expensive and time-consuming but just profitable enough to justify the expense. I've never been a big believer in the idea that you will somehow get brand recognition and goodwill in the community by attending the events. While I'm sure there is an element of truth to that, every time I heard someone repeat the refrain, in my mind, I was thinking, this is their way of saying this show sucks. The collective mindset reminded me of the old saying, "Why do people rob banks? Because that's where the money is." Unfortunately, there were too many people trying to rob the same banks. We needed to find the road less traveled and the bank less robbed.

In 2018, we began to introduce the idea of creating our own virtual events with vendors who served the same community. We would walk the convention floor handing out flyers highlighting the benefits of partnering with our company. The value proposition was simple—we provide the content, the speakers, and the creativity. All you need to do is promote it to your database of customers and allow us to use your logo in our promotional efforts. That was great because it provided credibility in the marketplace through implied endorsements. We had some success, but most of the folks we approached said while they loved the idea, it just felt like too much work, and they were so busy it didn't seem worth the effort. However, they appreciated the creativity, and once COVID hit, our concept suddenly made a lot of sense. These were folks who were used to being in front of doctors all the time at trade shows, in the practices and in-person training for their products and services. Once that was gone, there weren't many attractive alternatives to our idea. You couldn't spend marketing money if you wanted to; there was no place to spend it. The best part? Our solution was free. The silver lining in all this was that COVID forced many companies to re-think how they found and acquired new customers. Think about the math. We were spending approximately one million dollars annually to go to the shows.

As I mentioned before, the cost was a little over $10,000 per show—expensive but necessary at the time. Once the lockdowns began, there were *no* shows, *zero*. The net result was our marketing budget went from $83,000 a month to zero. To me, that's mind-blowing. I have never experienced such a rapid, dramatic shift in market dynamics in my life. It was exciting and terrifying at the same time. On the one hand, that's a huge savings for a company of our size. On the other hand, we needed a consistent stream of new acquisitions to grow. So, when it was all said and done, and people asked about the inspiration for many of these strategies, it was simple: necessity combined with a healthy dose of fear of failure.

One of our early COVID events included a prominent dermatologist, someone you would absolutely consider a KOL speaker. We had 300 people register and around 165 in attendance, which is good for free registration virtual events. We promoted his upcoming virtual event while teaching digital marketing best practices to attendees. It went well, but we had a long way to go in terms of refining the call to action, promotional consideration, etc. We did end up with a new customer from the event, and the cost was zero. *But that's not the best part.* In the early stages of the Zoom Boom, most of the industry was still new to the process, especially the doctors, surgeons, and associations. So, finding a partner to organize your event at short notice wasn't easy. We established a reputation for quality online programming in a very short period. I received a call from someone looking to host a virtual version of their annual meeting. That was a new twist as, technically, we weren't virtual event planners. When he told me the numbers he expected and the amount they were charging to attend their seven-hour production, I thought, "Oh, boy, all we have is a GoToWebinar account and a few events under our belt, but hey, that's more than they have; and the bonus is that we get to do a brief presentation to all the attendees." That would have been enough for me until the representative asked what we typically charged for full-day events. All I could think to say was, "I'm sorry, what was that you said?" We got to present *and* were paid, receiving more than we would typically *pay* to attend the event in person. We were on the board. The event went very well, and we had officially turned an expense into revenue. Said another way, we got paid to acquire customers, and of course, we ended up with the info from all attendees. That was lightning in a bottle, but it showed we were way past proof of concept, and virtual meetings as a source of new customers would become a mainstay of our marketing efforts for the foreseeable future.

The lesson here was, in the era of Zoom Boom, you can't steal second base and keep one foot on first. At some point, you have to go for it.

Going Once, Twice, SOLD

In 2020, two private equity groups approached us to purchase Crystal Clear outright. We were not for sale, although that is kind of a misleading statement as we were always for sale at the right price. Adam did what he does best, playing another great hand of poker with people who know how to play cards at the highest level. I have always admired his courage in high-stakes negotiations. Adam always said, "Every deal gets to a place where it's time to f--- off or walk," and no one is better at finding that sweet spot than Adam DeGraide. Our relationship had morphed over the years with many twists and turns. Disagreements, constant stress, and financial pressure will strain even the strongest relationships. I am grateful for my time together as Adam's partner and friend. He is off to the races again, starting another digital marketing and software company, and I have no doubt it will be another home run. After a one-year battle with cancer, Tommy is killing it in his new career. Between COVID, Tom getting sick, and shifting priorities of the partners, the timing of the sale could not have been better.

Like all partnerships, none are pretty, and none are perfect. Nor was ours. But Adam and I built and sold two very successful companies together, and I learned a valuable lesson from our sixteen-year relationship: everyone has a good beast and a bad beast, including myself, but you can't love half a person. Instead, you must accept both sides, learning to forgive when possible, and to love despite someone's shortcomings.

BIG NEWS

THIS JUST IN

CRYSTAL CLEAR RANKED

#210

ON THE 2018 INC. 500 LIST OF
FASTEST-GROWING PRIVATE
COMPANIES IN AMERICA!

2018 Inc. 500

Second time in the INC 500

Working the booth at Crystal Clear

Crystal Clear management team retreat to Catalina Island

Me and Tommy hangin at our favorite spot- The Cove, Atlantis, Bahamas

Loved traveling with Adam and Krystle

Celebrating at the INC 500 event in San Antonio

The three amigos- Me, Adam and Tommy

Giving back with Chad, Brittany, Bonnie and Ben

PART FOUR

FUTURE PLANS AND SOME REFLECTIONS

"Life can only be understood backwards; but it must be lived forwards." — Søren Kierkegaard

11

FUTURE PLANS

Here and Now

Family Update

My wife and children are all busy and doing well. Bonnie and I maintain close ties with our extended family, and our house is often the gathering place during holidays. I am going through a fourth transition, trying to decide what I want to do when I grow up. At the same time, Bonnie stays busy as executive director of Herren Project, a national nonprofit that assists families and individuals struggling with addiction. Herren Project hopes to break the stigma of addiction, bring positive awareness to the disease, and help to prevent substance use disorder. She is walking in purpose and loves her leadership role.

Bonnie's ability to be at home with our children through high school is an enormous source of pride for us both. In raising our children, we were a team and played our parts.

Chad, now 26, is in Orlando, working for PatientNOW as a software salesman. He has been part of the organization since college. A natural-born sales guy, leader, and public speaker, Chad gets it. Abigail, 24, has already passed her CPA and works as a corporate advisor for a global accounting firm. She was always the most disciplined and focused of the three growing up. Like Chad and Ben, Abigail is a natural-born leader. She lives in Philadelphia. Benjamin is a junior at the University of Rhode Island and is probably most like me in many ways. He is the fundraising chairperson for his fraternity. He is a very principled person and a good student, but he flirts with both beasts a bit more than the other two, so we're going to keep an eye on that. I remind him of the two beasts' story, and I am confident he will tame them. Part of me feels another start-up someday, and if I do, I would absolutely include Ben. The other two are too expensive at this point.

The Imposter and Adrenaline Junkie

So, life is good, and once again, I am facing new decisions about the trajectory of my life. I'm working on several projects right now. I am the host of two great podcasts, *True to Form*, which is related to elective medicine. The other podcast is *Right in Front of Me*, which explores the growing demand for skilled trade labor and the notion that every high school graduate is pushed to college for all the narrative despite skyrocketing tuition costs and exploding student loan debt. I have also started an educational platform to promote business and financial literacy for kids of all ages called SparkMoneyIQ. SparkMoneyIQ was created to educate, empower, and inspire students and future business leaders. I developed the platform in collaboration with a group of brilliant Rhode Island DECA students.

I still struggle with living in the moment and enjoying the fruits of our labor. It drives my wife crazy because when people ask me about my track record as an entrepreneur, sometimes I say things like, "Oh, you know, you catch a break here or there," or "You get lucky." She says, "I hope you don't self-deprecate in the book, honey. People want to know how you did it, and it is insulting to answer them that way." But I still feel like an imposter at times and could write a whole chapter about how that feeling followed me through my job at the bank and subsequent start-ups. I was always afraid that someone would "out" the real me, the bad beast inside, so I had to work even harder to prove myself. I often find myself wandering around my home thinking, wow, these people have a nice place. I know that does not sound normal, but what part of this book sounds normal?

I have some deferred maintenance to deal with in my emotional and physical health, the result of an extended period of singular focus. And then there is the adrenaline level you function with when trying to accomplish big goals. For example, suppose you need to bring in a million dollars a month to keep your business going. In that case, there is a lot of adrenaline associated with that as the person primarily responsible for bringing in the money. After years of running a sales team, the adrenaline does not disappear once the business is sold. You are stuck with all the energy and velocity your mind needs to function at that level, but you have lost the outlet for all that energy. I'm handling it better this time around. I am grateful for the opportunity to write this book and hope it will make a difference in some small way. If just one person is meaningfully impacted, it will be worth it.

Future Goals

Working with High School Students

My idea of working with high school students began when I met John Shepard. John is the founder of the STRAC Institute, an electronics trade school he started primarily to help service-disabled veterans. John, a veteran himself, started the company with the idea of helping veterans transition out of the military into meaningful civilian employment. The military would pay for the training, and John's company would prepare them for a career in electronics, providing training and thirteen certifications to lead them into well-paying jobs. STRAC is now open to everyone, veterans and non-veterans. When I met some of the students and saw the impact STRAC had on them, I wanted to see if I could help spread the word. That is how the podcast, *Right in Front of Me* started. It connects "vets of all ages, high school graduates, and career changers looking for long-term opportunities in the exciting world of electronics." It connects you with "the hot topics, employers, educators, military personnel, and everyday people making a difference in the world of vocational training. We have done about fifteen episodes to date.

Students today are usually taught that if they don't go to college, they will be losers, but if you look at the unintended consequences, we will pile up more debt. There is $1.7 trillion in student debt, which is more than the total outstanding credit card debt in the United States. I hope to help change that by teaching students basic financial, business, and entrepreneurial skills, mainly through instruction. I started a parent company named Profit for Intent because it will be a for-profit business designed to do good first and make money second. By "do good," I mean there will be some tangible benefit other than selling something. Anything I do going forward will have a dual purpose.

Forgiveness and Giving Back

My last two goals are important on emotional and spiritual levels. First, I want to be comfortable with that guy in the mirror. I may never get there, but I'll keep trying. I have been hurt by those I cared about, and I have caused more than my fair share of hurt. Second, I need to remember that we are all just humans and that everyone contains good beasts and bad beasts. Failing to forgive those who have wronged us can keep us tied up in anger, which leads to destructive behavior. Failing to forgive ourselves has the same result. It has sometimes led to my thoughts of living my life as an imposter, as someone who does not deserve personal and professional prosperity.

To forgive is to set a prisoner free and discover that the prisoner was you. –Lewis B. Smedes

My goal of giving back, at this point, includes supporting Bonnie's work at the Herren Project. We just gave $50,000 for the end-of-the-year fundraiser. Last year, we donated 100% of her after-tax salary, which means she works about 70 hours a week for free. She is grateful for the opportunity to make a difference in the world; going forward we will donate ten percent of any book revenue to the Herren Project.

Mom, Dad, me, Tommy and Todd

Chad, Abby and Ben outside our home in RI

Dad, Tom, me and Todd

I love you Bonnie

The Sawyer side of the family at my Dad's house

12

SOME REFLECTIONS

I am in my early 50s and have experienced four major turning points in my life, learning valuable lessons and personal insights along the way.

Reflecting on my life, especially my priorities, has always been a valuable and important exercise for me since I am wired to move quickly and sometimes on impulse. Some of my thoughts, beliefs, and conclusions may not echo yours, and that's OK. That's what makes this world beautiful.

- Most people in the throes of addiction are inherently good. They are not the bad things they do; those bad things are mainly a function of their addiction. They are trying to feed that beast, but it doesn't mean they do not want to be good. Unfortunately, they lose their way from time to time, me included.

- It may seem strange, but I am grateful for what I went through as a teenager. I don't know anyone who looks back on their teen years and thinks everything went perfectly. We all made mistakes, and we learned something from them. The most important lesson I learned from my experience is that I have the capacity to do terrible things to myself and others. I have the capacity to be a thief, a compulsive liar, an addict, and self-destructive to the point of flirting with my own mortality, to hurt those I love, to be manipulative, and all the other "isms" associated with my self-discovery and inventory. Those capacities are scary because, at the core, I am still the same person I was at fifteen, so I will struggle the rest of my life to feed the good beast inside rather than the bad.

- One of the worst things I have done has been to judge Christianity by the behavior of Christians. People are fallible. That's why we need to have faith.

- If you want people to follow you, you must earn their trust. Through words and deeds. You have to say, "I need you to help me." Never invoke the name or authority of someone else. Be willing to do whatever you have to do to help them and put them in a position to win. Otherwise, you lose respect—your children won't listen to you, and your employees won't follow you.

- On being an entrepreneur: The willingness to learn, persevere, and take risks are paramount to sustainable success. You must have an extremely high tolerance for risk, and if you are in a relationship, your partner must have the same tolerance or be able to trust you implicitly. You also need to understand *why* you want to become an entrepreneur and precisely what you are signing up for because you will become disappointed and disillusioned at times. You must realize that being at the top means everything is your problem.

- Strong leadership and trust will go a long way, and taking responsibility for your actions is an integral part of that equation. Taking responsibility and ownership is how you begin to solve problems. If you live your life saying, "It's my dad's fault," or "I got a bad break," it's a crutch, an excuse to return to bad behavior. If you say to me, "My business is bad because my employees are terrible," I will ask you, "Who hired them?" or say, "Maybe it is because you are a bad boss."

- Appreciate the support of those close to you. No man is an island. There's never been a significant business decision I've made without consulting my father, as he can offer not only business acumen but an outside observer's perspective. He would be there to talk me off a ladder when I was upset, with words like, "If you put it in perspective, Tim, or if you look at what could have happened." He was able to squeeze the anger and emotion out of an argument or conversation by saying, "Tim, let's think this through for a second. The kids are all doing great, and you have a beautiful wife." He helped me focus on the issue at hand, and then the solution would reveal itself.

- It is essential to take time out to revisit your goals and reassess your life's path. I do a lot of introspective thinking and am in a constant state of analysis. During my first job, with the bank, I worked all the time to achieve material success, consumed with the need for more and more to validate my self-worth. I was trapped in a vicious cycle, becoming increasingly unhappy but not knowing how to stop it.
- If you surround yourself with like-minded people, you are missing out. When I took my family on a cross-country RV trip, it provided all of us with a different perspective on the world and the people in it. Get out, travel, and broaden your mind by learning from others who are not of your race, culture, or religion.
- There is no permanent state of being in life, no permanently bad things or good things. It is never fatal until it's fatal.
- Don't hide your past, especially from your children. If you did some things that you're not proud of, that's OK. For me, the best way to shape the future was through sharing my past. It always amazes me when I hear people judge others for doing things they themselves did at one point in time.
- If there is something in your professional life that cripples you, you need to deal with it. When you conquer what you fear most, it can become one of the things that you most cherish and value. My fear of public speaking is a

prime example. Although I still become nervous before speaking, I love it.

- "It's all McDonald's." Jim Gaffigan, a comedian, talks about how culturally it is no longer cool to go to McDonald's, although they are busier than ever before. Jim does a skit about a man who goes into McDonald's and sees a friend there who says, "What are you doing here?" The man answers, "Oh, I'm not getting lunch or anything. I'm just waiting for a friend," who he then discloses is a male hooker. Nothing will make him admit that he wants to eat there. The point of the skit is that people say, "Well, yea I do this, but I would never do that." Overeating, binge-watching TV, constant scrolling on your phone, overworking, porn, drugs, alcohol— it's all McDonald's. It is all one-upmanship, a need to feel better than others or superior, and we all do it. Jim Gaffigan says,

I'm tired of people acting like they're better than McDonald's. It's like you may have never set foot in McDonald's, but you have your own McDonald's. Maybe instead of buying a Big Mac, you read US Weekly. Hey, that's still McDonald's. It is just served up a little differently. Maybe your McDonald's is telling yourself that Starbucks Frappuccino is not a milkshake. It's all McDonald's— McDonald's of the soul: momentary pleasure followed by incredible guilt, eventually leading to cancer—

We are all just people trying to do the best we can with what we have. A little grace can go a long way. A good friend once told me, "Holding back forgiveness is like drinking poison and hoping the other guy dies." So, send some love today; make that call, shoot that long-overdue text. And above all else, *love yourself*.

If you made it this far, thank you for listening to my story. I am not ashamed of my journey and am proud to no longer be hiding. If any part of my story speaks to you, I hope it gives you the strength to overcome your beasts and to stop your own version of hiding. We are all imperfect, with two beasts within us. And remember to ask yourself, which beast are you feeding?

Cheers,

Tim

There are no words to express my gratitude for my wife, my family and friends made along the way